Unconditional Love -The High Side of Life

A Love-Linked Life Story

Keith Turnbull

UNCONDITIONAL LOVE
The High Side of Life

Ever since our marriage 63 years ago, Sally has sent
Christmas cards celebrating the birth of Jesus and her love
for you. Her final encouragement message to you is to live a
life of Unconditional Love.

Keith and Sally Turnbull

Edited and Designed by Jessica T Weaver

Book Cover design by Felix Erman Yudi

Original Photographs by Cassady K Photography

Kent Van Horn photo credit to Case Alumnus Magazine

Jack Wallace photo credit to Case Western Alumni Association

ISBN: 978-0-578-77475-6

First Edition: October 2020

www.unconditionallovethebook.com

Contents

Foreword

Unconditional Love tells a life story so compelling yet features Keith and Sally Turnbull, who are ordinary and humble people. By the grace of God and an unwavering commitment to live their lives according to God's principles, they have not only experienced great "success" in life, but, more importantly, they have left an indelible mark of unconditional love on the lives of countless others.

Therefore, dear reader, please know that this life story is the real thing. It is a story that encourages you to seek the high side of life in all your endeavors, then gives you an instruction manual to get you started.

I first met Keith and Sally Turnbull 34 years ago at a church my wife and I had started attending, Allegheny Center Alliance Church, on the North Side of Pittsburgh. They invited us to their home on a Sunday afternoon along with dozens of other young adults to their "backyard," a seven-acre lake with a myriad of pre-designed entertainment possibilities. But the extraordinary part was that the Turnbulls repeated this gathering every Sunday! Expecting nothing in return, their sole purpose was to welcome young adults at our church and to shower them with love. Lunch was prepared for all who attended. The house was intentionally understated, all to handle the volume of visitors without concern for wear and tear. Meanwhile, unbeknownst to me at the time, Keith was busy as a rising executive in a multi-national corporation.

I found myself asking about Keith and Sally Turnbull, "Who are these two?" It was a question I asked many times over the years as I witnessed the extraordinary manner and circumstances in which they loved all kinds of people. Family and friends, career or church, whatever the context of one's connection to the Turnbulls, rest assured they would give you encouragement, support and love.

In addition to wondering "Who," I also found myself asking, "Why?" Why aren't Keith and Sally content to enjoy their success and live out the American Dream? Why do they habitually pour into the lives of others, expecting nothing in return? For the Turnbulls, this is all part of the high side of life. It can be for you and me as well!

When I later joined the pastoral staff of ACAC, I experienced this dynamic first-hand, as Keith, who was by then recently retired, began to almost surreptitiously mentor me in various aspects of leadership and organizational dynamics. These lessons almost always came back to the guiding principles about the value people bring to every endeavor we undertake. Over time, I grew to love and to respect this man even more than I had previously, and to welcome his insights.

We have also had the chance to put some of Keith's counterintuitive approaches into practice in specific ministry settings at ACAC. Our Food Ministry has had a dramatic transformation in its capacity to better serve all the people and ministries of our church. This ministry success story, which Keith outlines as a practical case study in the appendix to his book, led me to ask Keith to write a book. But as he began to engage the project, he realized that the story he needed to tell was much bigger than the one I was asking for. Thankfully, he followed his own instincts; *Unconditional Love - The High Side of Life,* is the result.

If you want to live a life filled with God-honoring purpose and meaning, this story is for you!

If you want to consider the life principles upon which real success is founded, this story is for you!

If you want to leave behind a legacy of unconditional love among those you care about, this story is for you!

God wants nothing less for you than the high side of life. Keith and Sally Turnbull's story is the tale of a couple who sought for it... and found it. I trust it will do more than just encourage you. I trust it will help you find it, too.

-Blaine Workman
Administrative Pastor
Allegheny Center Alliance Church

Introduction

When I was growing up in the 1940s, my first paid job was a newspaper route. Every afternoon, the paper man dropped off a bundle of 29 papers at the corner of Detroit and Wagar Roads in Rocky River, Ohio and I would deliver them to my customers, regardless of the weather conditions. My pay was a penny per paper.

One day as I was on my bike delivering papers, I saw a girl on her bike delivering papers on an adjacent paper route. I had of course seen girls my whole life, but something different happened this time. I had no idea who she was at the time but somehow my "seeing" was changed. It was not this way when I saw Nancy Jones and Roberta Turner, the two girls with whom I played baseball.

Then I saw this girl a second time on Elmwood Hill. We had fresh snow on the hill, so I hurried there after my paper route with my steel runner sled. There she was, sledding down the hill. I was never schooled in boy-girl etiquette and did not quite know how to meet her. But I wanted to. So the next time she ran down the hill to get a fast start and jumped onto her sled, I did the same thing. I then caught up with her, grabbed the back runner of her sled and spun her sled around sideways. It was what we boys did to each other. We called it ditching.

Well, it did work. I got to talk to this girl, but not on friendly terms. She had a very different opinion of ditching than my friends Jim Kemp and Carl Laco had. And she certainly told me how much she disliked being ditched. I later learned she was what we called a tomboy – a girl very skilled in sports, so much so that she sought excellence such as "king of the hill," an avid sled rider.

Oh well, I was still attracted to her. My first approach to her was a bit flawed. So I asked for advice from a girl I knew and tried with Sally again, and again, and again. Sally and I have now been married 63 years and are deeply in love.

Read on, as Sally and I have a life story worth sharing that we've written with honesty and uncommon candor. We have intentionally revealed "Learning Lessons" as our story progresses, so that you can read and use (if you choose to) some of the lessons in your own life story. We have been married 63 years, sharing a deep love that has never wavered. We love the Lord, and He has blessed our family to grow from two to 55 (and still growing). We are intentionally writing to our 20 grandchildren and their 12 spouses (so far) who have 11 great-grandchildren (so far), and of course, we are writing to you.

As a family, we love, intentionally bond, and seek time with one another. I was poor and then Sally and I became wealthy. We are both humble, such that it is not easy to write a book about successes. But we have shared our testimony and wisdom with our family, church, and others for decades; at bible study, at our yearly camping trip, etc. and we strive to record our story for future generations in this book.

I prepared to become a research scientist, but then became an executive vice president in business. I had ten different jobs in Alcoa. I was aggressively mentored in nine of them and deeply admired all of my mentors. My seventh job had no mentor because the job had never been done before. My tenth job was mentored by a master teacher (a sensei) that Toyota had brought to develop an American supply base.

Sally and I became Christians in unusual ways that profoundly impacted our lives. Sally taught 5th grade girls at church for over 50 years. Sally is an encourager; she imparted love to every girl she taught. We bought a lake for our family, only to learn that it was God's lake where He intended to show His love. We had an open house at our home for teens and young adults from our church every Sunday afternoon for about 15 years, with a typical attendance of 35. Sally is a prolific writer sending out encouraging notes virtually every day and 750 at Christmas. Our children, grandchildren and their spouses are all Christians, striving to live their life stories well.

Our family and my close friend Blaine Workman asked me to write. Therefore, I wrote a candid version of the life story Sally and I share, with Sally's insights; and with my granddaughter Jessica Weaver's journalism skills. I repeat that our humility made this book difficult to write. But love mandated that we write it.

Our story is 120 years long, beginning with our parents who shaped our lives, and then extending to the year 2020 when I am 85 and Sally is 84. We have chosen three persistent themes - God, Family and Career - about which to write because they individually and collectively reveal the essence of our lives. Then, in each era of our lives, we point out the key principles or insights we are engaging. Why? Because it is easier for you to move whatever you find meritorious from our life to yours if you apply the principle, rather than the detailed story imbedded within our backgrounds, which may differ from yours. We pray for you to learn the high side - getting closer to the principle as God designed it.

I am honored that you would consider reading my book. Time is precious, books are plentiful and social media is enticing. However, I dare to encourage you to read on, because the stories that I share can impact your life. Every word I've written, and every experience I share, is presented such that you can use it as an addendum to your life story. You do not have to live like Sally or me; such would be an absurd imposition. Our intent is to be helpful, whomsoever you are and howsoever you are living.

1

Our Roots

The Roaring Twenties - 1900 to 1930

My great-grandparents emigrated from Scotland and England, and settled in Cleveland, Ohio. Sally's are from Germany and settled in McComb, Ohio. They grew up in a robust period that impacted the life story of Sally and me greatly.

Both Sally's parents and mine grew up by the 1920's, married and then had their first child. Bill Ewing was born to Sally's parents in 1926 and Bruce Turnbull was born to Keith's parents in 1928. It was the "Roaring Twenties" after World War I had ended in 1918. Both fathers, Bob Ewing and Gordon Turnbull, had been too young to fight in the war. Both families were busy and prospering; the Ewings as an accountant and schoolteacher who had moved into a newly built house in 1929, and the Turnbulls as farmers with a large farm who had moved into a newly built house. Both families were churchgoers to Protestant churches. The Ewings had moved from McComb to Rocky River and into their home one mile away from the Turnbulls. Both sets of parents in the Roaring Twenties were experiencing the euphoria of a booming, overconfident, and we-are-smarter-than-God society.

- Farms and businesses were succeeding.
- Liquor became prohibited by law in 1920.
- "Speakeasys" served liquor as a blatant rejection of law.
- Churches were becoming "enlightened" - deciding that the Bible is neither accurate nor inspired.
- Churches split into "enlightened" or "fundamental."
- "Fundamentalists" were the minority – Turnbulls attended there.
- "Enlightened" kept the church buildings – Ewings stayed there.
- The period was really roaring – much hype.
- The liquor prohibition law thereafter was repealed in 1933.
- Our situations with God, Family and Careers were all poised for huge change!

Summary so far: Both families are intact with vocations, their first child, a new home and Roaring Twenties gusto. Their risk thus far are their:

- o   Church – separating into liberal and conservative
- o   Families – both seem to be intact
- o   Career – all four parents seem to be strong and secure

The Great Depression: 1930 to 1940

In 1930, the stock markets crashed, banks collapsed, and the Great Depression engulfed the nation for 10 years. Our brothers – Bruce Turnbull and Bill Ewing – were born before the Great Depression and Sally and I were born in the middle of the Great Depression (1936 and 1935).

Turnbulls

The transition from Roaring Twenties to Great Depression was massive. My grandparents – John and Jennie Turnbull – lost their large farm and house to back taxes but were allowed to stay in the house temporarily because my grandmother was near death. I write this from my brother's recollections because I was too young to remember this grandmother and I only slightly remember this grandfather. My parents had built their house on my grandparents' farm so they also lost their house when the farm was lost. We moved into a rental house and my grandfather moved in with us after my grandmother died. Our rental house was on a main road, so we hung out a tourist sign on our front porch to take in overnight guests to help pay our rent. I would give up my room if a tourist stopped by. Sometimes the tourists stayed and stayed. Carrie Hudnut came along as a tourist and then stayed until she died several years later. My mother cared for her in the years that her health deteriorated. She was then followed by Frank and Vi McLane who came as two-week tourists and then stayed for decades – long beyond my graduation from college.

These stark changes – farmers without a farm and homeowners without their houses – were shaping my life. We were now compressed into half of a double house that we must sublet to tourists and we are going to our conservative church that had separated from the "enlightened" Protestant church.

The first church I remember was a fundamental Baptist church in a rented storefront with about ten attendees and no pastor. Mrs. Wildy, my Sunday school teacher, taught me about Jesus and I believed and accepted Christ as my Savior when I was about seven years old. I was overwhelmed with joy and rushed out to share my faith with others.

Unfortunately, she packaged several of her conservative non-church views into her salvation message such as no movies, no liquor, no smoking, etc. Therefore, my brother who went to the movies and my father who smoked and drank were (by her teaching) going to hell. She was wrong, but I did not know that until age 12. I was exposed to ridicule, teasing and sometimes physical abuse whenever I shared her salvation message with others. It took years for me to finally separate from her amplified presentation the simple core truth of salvation – that sinners are saved by believing that Jesus died on the cross to redeem us from our sins. After a five-year-long internal debate about the extra rules proposed by Mrs. Wildy, I finally attended a movie, Walt Disney's Dumbo, and separated the truth of salvation from the distractions. I felt relieved to know the truth of salvation – God's unconditional love for me - now without the baggage.

My father and grandfather were particularly impacted by the trauma of loss and the ten years of national chaos during the Great Depression. Both tended to be stubborn, a trait that likely intensified in harmful ways during these tense years of their lives. For instance, my parents asked my grandfather to separate off a lot from his farm so that they would own the property upon which they built their house. But my grandfather refused and stubbornly resisted changing his mind. So, when my grandfather lost his farm from back taxes, my parents lost their house too.

Thereafter, such stubbornness also showed up in my father, which was painful in the long term. When I was about five years old, a pastor from Elyria Baptist Church came to visit my grandfather and they got into an argument that my father overheard. My father became so upset that he decided to never attend church again, a vow that he constrained himself to for my childhood and then almost to his death at age 68. He maintained his faith and listened to a sermon every Sunday on the radio but refused to darken a church door. This stubbornness also alienated him from his extended family – his sister and his wife's family – in part because he also drank and smoked. His faith in God was strong but he was held hostage by his stubbornness.

By the time he was in his 60s, he had held rigidly to the "I won't go to church" decision for decades, until he remarried following my mother's death. His new wife Marge learned that my brother had graduated from seminary, and was preaching at a nearby church, but my father had never heard him. She shouted at him "That's the stupidest thing I've ever heard! You and I are going to church to hear him!" She was shocked that his stubbornness had constrained him from hearing his son. So they went, and thereafter attended church regularly.

There was a time during the Great Depression when my father moved out from our home to an apartment a mile away. I was too young to remember that and my mother protected us from the situation. But Bruce told me about it and said my parents reunited after a few months because it would be important for Bruce and me. My father was a hard worker and loved me, but this disregard of his family was costly. I learned early in life that his decisions were nonnegotiable, so I asked permission from him for things that I did not care much about and asked my mother's permission for important things.

Look ahead to the time of my mother's death and my parents' love had deepened such that my father was devastated by her sudden death during cancer surgery. I was loved by my mother and father always. I have written about these early years of my life not to belittle my parents, but to share the harsh Great Depression conditions during which God shaped me.

Feltons and Rogers

My maternal grandparents, Tom and Frances Felton, had English roots and lived on the east side of Cleveland where my grandfather was a City Councilman. By the time I was born, they had moved from their city location to a west-side country location with a ten-acre farm including two houses, a barn and a small greenhouse. They were proud that their predecessor in England had been "florist to the King of England." Their greenhouse and farm carried forward their florist roots. During the Great Depression, they did not lose their farm. As they saw the pain of the Great Depression in their community, they repurposed large portions of their farm so people suffering from hunger could have garden plots to grow vegetables at no cost. My grandfather and grandmother lived in the eastern house and my Aunt Dorothy, Uncle Lynn, and their five children lived in the western house. Then death struck during the Great Depression.

Uncle Lynn, the man in the far-right side of the below photo, died from a heart attack at age 43. Aunt Dorothy became a widow with five children. Thereafter, my grandfather Tom, the man farthest left in the photo, suffered a severe stroke and was bedridden for years. He was cared for by family at home, but never in a hospital.

Felton grandparents, Aunt and Uncle Rogers and five Roger cousins in 1939

My cousin Bob, the tall teen in the center, was the second born and the eldest male cousin. While in high school at age 16, he became "the father" after my grandfather's stroke; attending school, working as a school janitor for income and learning to lead the family. He became so proficient that when World War II began, the draft board exempted him from going to war because of his critical role as "father" at home.

Meanwhile, my mother May had her house full with her husband, two sons, my grandfather and tourists. She lived three miles away from her sister by bus.

We were poised to discover "cousins" not as a genetic word, but as a love-linked lifestyle to navigate depression / death / stroke. That love-linked lifestyle is a pervasive person-to-person environment in which selfishness is driven to near zero in a person. Then, a whole set of people sense each other's needs and sacrifice to meet that need. This environment was created by my strong and selfless mother, who was the role model for Sally to later create a family that loves and works together.

We were poised to discover "cousins" not as a genetic word, but as a love-linked lifestyle to navigate depression/death/stroke.

The two aunts - my mother and her sister - closed ranks so they could provide the in-home-perpetual care my grandfather required after his stroke. In that era of the late 1930s, most families had no car or one car, because two cars would have been an extravagance. Therefore, my mother and I traveled back and forth by bus as the seven cousins merged together as though we were brothers and sisters. Aunt Dorothy could not afford her house on her own, so she and her five children moved into the small three-bedroom house of our grandparents. It worked. It really did work. Love abounded, everyone pitched in, the cows were milked, the chickens were fed, the hogs were butchered, the farm was plowed, and the crops were harvested. All of this happened while six cousins were in school and I was the preschool bus rider with my mother.

Of great significance, church now became a Cousin experience as Aunt Dorothy and we seven cousins went to

Rogers cousins

church together. All of the boys except me went on to become pastors. My mother supported us but stayed home with our father on Sunday mornings to share the radio sermon he had chosen. All seven of us were discipled as Christians as we grew up in Grayton Road Baptist Church under exemplary pastors, Pastor Nicka and Pastor Willetts.

My mother was a kind, loving and caring woman with very little money. She sacrificially supported her ill sister who had five children. Yet my mother saw people with needs and gave them what she had. Items were constantly disappearing from our house because someone else such as the mailman needed them more than we did. I have never seen a more generous person than my mother. She gave herself away too. I have no doubt that the saving of her marriage (by whatever terms she worked out with our father) was so that Bruce and I would be a family again. Those acts of love caused our father to love her intensely by the time she died. Love grew in their marriage.

To seal this assertion of deepening love, I'll take you temporarily out of our time sequence to the year 1963 to see the role my niece Martha played in my parents' love story. Their first granddaughter Martha (Bruce's daughter) incurred blood trauma immediately after birth that severely damaged her cerebrum, the part of the brain that governs motion. She was smart but had almost no muscle control; a rag doll requiring perpetual care. She could not even intentionally swallow what you put in her mouth. Her care was extensive and involved many people. By the time she was 11 years old, she was living with my parents who became Martha's sole providers, working collaboratively to meet her needs and to isolate her from the health risks inherent in taking her outside their home. They both loved Martha deeply and could read her desires and needs despite her inability to speak, including which TV programs Martha liked or didn't like.

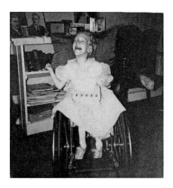

Martha in 1961

When my mother was diagnosed with stomach cancer in 1963, their protective cocoon for Martha was breached as my mother needed surgery. I had to call my brother Bruce in Cedarville, Ohio and tell him to quickly drive the 180 miles to Cleveland because our mother was at risk of dying of surgery complications. He left immediately but when he arrived, I had to tell him that both our mother and Martha had died only a few hours apart. It was front page news in the Cleveland newspaper, a love story with nearly simultaneous deaths.

We were all in shock, but I had my wife and three kids to stave off the loneliness from my mother's death. But the very essence of my father's love life had been stripped away. He knew my mother and Martha were saved and now in heaven, relieved of handicaps and pain, but he and they had become one and he was intensely in love with both of them. I focused on the task of clearing out their house, which my father never returned to. Bruce and his wife Eleanor, and Sally and I had just learned an incredible life story about the ways love grows when we treat each other as God intends, with unconditional love. My mother was a selfless caregiver, and my father was a hard worker, which brought them together in Martha's care and expanded my father's love for my mother.

World War II: 1941 to 1945

Now, moving back in time from the 1963 Martha story, let us return to the seven cousins drawn together during the Great Depression and World War II. The United States did not want to go to war just 20 years after "the War to End All Wars," but such was not to be. Japan invaded us at Pearl Harbor in 1941. We then declared war on Japan, and Germany declared war on us two weeks later. The entire nation closed ranks in support of the war effort, a unity unlike any you have ever seen.

Keith's Story

At the age of six, I saw the war primarily through the eyes of my parents and my cousins (Janet, Bob, Carol, Lynn Jr. and Frances) and my brother Bruce. Janet's husband Ken Rockenstein was draft age but failed his physical exam, so he spent the war building airplanes in a Cleveland plant staffed mostly with women. Carol's fiancé Wilbur Pincombe served in the infantry and survived the battle for Saipan Island in the Southern Pacific in June 1944 during which 3,000 Americans died and 13,000 were wounded. About 27,000 Japanese died in the battle. The Saipan civilians were warned that the American troops would kill them, so thousands leapt to their deaths from high cliffs. In early 1945, Wilbur went next to the 82-day battle for Okinawa Island in which 12,500 Americans, about 100,000 Japanese and about 100,000 Okinawa civilians were killed. Bob Rogers was exempted from the draft because of his father role. The other men were all too young to be drafted. Fifty-two million people died in World War II; one of them was Dick Folke, our next-door neighbor. The war effort drew our nation together into an industrial giant; making tanks, airplanes, ships and weapons, mostly by women. Our cousins drew together even tighter as we prayed for the safety of Wilbur and for the end of this horrific war. The Christmas song "*I'll be Home for Christmas ... if only in my dreams*" took on a new meaning for the Rogers/Turnbull family as we sang, prayed, and yearned for his return home.

And then, he did return. Our family member came home. First, the Germans unconditionally surrendered at the end of a bloody invasion all the way to Berlin. Thereafter, our Allied forces were closing in upon Japan for another bloody invasion. But we dropped an atomic bomb and several days later, a second atomic bomb, whereupon Japan surrendered. Wilbur came home from the South Pacific, spared by not having to invade Japan. He and Carol married immediately. Sally and I had not yet met, but at age nine and ten years old, we had already learned that life is fragile, and love is precious.

We greeted the returning soldiers with joy and relief. However, the Turnbulls became caught up in the nationwide issue of lack of housing for soldiers back from the war. Due to the housing shortage, the government offered incentives to homeowners to convert a single home into a double, or a double home into a quadruple home, and the government would pay all of the conversion costs. We were in a rented double that our landlord wanted to convert. But, to do such work, we would have to leave. We were evicted at the very time when no housing was available. My mother drove up and down streets with me, looking for houses with no curtains in the windows, with the hope that it might be unoccupied. The search seemed to last forever for a nine-year-old like me and it proved to be a futile quest. The only vacant house we found was a 110-year-old abandoned farmhouse with a roof that had partially fallen in. We called the owner who lived in Buffalo, NY, explained our problem, and pleaded with him. "May we live here for one year if we repair it to liveable?" He said yes, so we mended the missing roof sections by replacing the wooden rafter beams and roof boards and covering those with tar paper. Then we moved into the house that had only cold water and electricity. Our kitchen sink had a hand pump instead of a faucet because we had to pump in water from an underground cistern that stored rainwater that we collected from our roof. The toilet was an outhouse so chamber pots were for overnight use; we moved lightbulbs from room to room to keep the occupied room lit; the stove was a wood burner; and the bathtub was a 24" steel tub we placed on the kitchen floor, because the only hot water was a kettle sitting on the stove. Every week or two, we would go to our cousins' house to experience the treat of a "real" bathtub.

The restored Cup and Saucer house

The floor joists sagged, and some had broken, rotted out by years of rain pouring into the house. My father cut down trees about 8" in diameter that he put in the basement to hold up the floor. He would jack up a joist to level, cut the tree to proper length and place it under the joist. We had so many such posts that we called the basement "the forest." We had a coal furnace that heated only the first floor. My bedroom was on the second floor so I used numerous blankets and dashed downstairs in the morning so that I could dress where it was warm.

But we were thrilled to have a roof over our heads. Our long-term tourists Frank and Vi McLane moved in with us as well, and after one year, we bought the house for $5,000. The house sat on an acre of fertile land and my father farmed every inch of it. He grew everything imaginable – blueberries, peaches, turnips, grapes, raspberries, corn, peas – and sold them to the local supermarket. The strawberry crop, sold at 50 cents a quart, paid our real estate taxes.

I was now 10 years old, a Christian, loved and bonded uncommonly well with my five cousins, all of whom were thrilled to have family and friends returned from the war. Meanwhile, Sally, who I have not yet met, describes her life story through the Great Depression and World War II.

Sally's Story

My story through age nine parallels Keith's in several ways. We also were seriously impacted by the Great Depression and World War II. My brother Bill was born June 6, 1926 to Bob and Mary Ewing who bought a new brick home at 21373 Stratford Avenue in Rocky River, OH where Bill and I lived until we went off to the war (for Bill) and to college (for Sally). My folks were from an upper middle-class family. Dad initially owned and operated five dining car restaurants on the west side of Cleveland. But due to the Great Depression, he lost all but one.

The one remaining was opposite Midland Steel in Lakewood where workers had the operation open 24/7 so Dad had plenty of business by staying open the same hours and employing excellent Hungarian cooks.

When the war came along, Bill had reached draft age but was not drafted until the very end of the war. He never saw active combat, but to finish his requirements, he managed a hotel in freshly liberated Paris until the war was over and he came back home to Rocky River. He had met a lovely girl, Jean White, who had been working at the Pentagon during the war, and they got married.

In such hard times in the world as I was born into, we still had memorable growing up events. Another little girl was born at the same time as I was: Shirley Temple, a child actress in the movies. Since I looked so much like Shirley, Mom dressed me like her, even rolling my blond hair into curls just like Shirley had. When I was about four or five years old, my parents were going to Florida and I cut off one of my front lovely curls. Mom cried over what I had done, so I cried, too. We went to Florida anyway, but with a large curl missing from the front of my face.

Actress Shirley Temple and Sally in 1947

It seemed like Dad was always working long hours when I was young, so Mom, a stay-at-home mother, was always reminding me to be quiet during his nap time each afternoon when he would take a break from his businesses. He also spent about a year recovering from a nervous breakdown with some time initially spent in the hospital. He was an absentee father, but we adjusted to it as a family.

I do recall cutting wood with Dad, though. He had an X-shaped wooden holder called a saw horse he made from a tree branch, and we would cut firewood-sized pieces on it with a two-man hand saw (chain saws hadn't been invented yet) into useable size for our living room fireplace. I loved cutting our front and back yards with the hand push mower, as gas or electric mowers were not invented yet. Bill was a loving brother to me. He built a cart on wheels to pull behind his bike, and I got to ride in it when I was preschool age.

My early childhood home was warm and welcoming and had a neat little box built into the side of our stairs to the second floor. I kept all of my toys in that "hole in the wall," so toys were never strewn about. I liked my breakfast nook in our kitchen where we ate, too. Cozy. I didn't like dolls except for my Teddy Bear (so named for an American president, Theodore Roosevelt). I still have it.

Bill got a German police dog when I was born, but Ginger became my close companion growing up since she was docile and allowed me to dress her in doll clothes. Mom would take Ginger and me for a daily walk either around the block where we lived, or along the Nickle Plate Railroad tracks that ran along the back of our property. I loved those walks. Ginger died of old age at 14 years old. Mom tried to buy a replacement collie for me, but that dog turned out so shy that it just stayed under the car all the time and we gave her back to the pet shop finally. Mom always wore a dress and low heels, rarely slacks.

Both sets of my grandparents were born and raised their families in McComb, Ohio, a small farming town. But my parents moved about 100 miles away to the Rocky River neighborhood near Cleveland, Ohio before I was born. My dad had one older sister, Joyce, and his dad owned a successful furniture business in town. My mom's family William and Almira Grose and their seven children lived just outside of town with the railroad running behind their home too. The train came by regularly to pick up grain and other farm items from the silos. Behind my grandma's home was a mulberry tree – which they thought was very messy when it bore fruit, but I loved the berries – and I still love mulberries! None of the cousins were my age except my mother's sister's two girls, who were rather close in age but a tad older: Marty and Libby Wasson. They also had an older brother about Bill's age named Bob. Roland and Ruth Wasson, my uncle and aunt, lived in McComb as well, so every Memorial Day, we'd all gather and kids would ride trikes and bikes decorated with red, white and blue streamers from the town to the close by (about ½ mile) cemetery. I loved decorating my trike spokes with the streamers. My family was a tightly connected mother, father, brother, and me. Our primary contacts with our neighbors were through me to those who had like-age children. We occasionally attended the Enlightened Protestant church. As World War II ended, we were poised to move into the Penguin Ice Cream era.

***

This life story segment that Sally wrote here differs from mine in many ways, but the trauma of the Great Depression and the War shaped our families and careers by the time we were nine and ten years old. Both families are engaged with God, but differently.

Before moving forward from the Great Depression and War periods, I have summarized some key Learning Lessons that were shaping our life stories and became foundational for all that is to follow. They are 67 statements worthwhile for you to read because some could be potentially useful in your own life story.

Learning Lessons:

Gordon and May (Felton) Turnbull side

God:

- Salvation has a sound core – adding baggage is bad.
- People divide the church – division is hard.
- People add onto the core – that can be painful.
- God is supreme – He rescued me from the baggage.

Family:

- Trauma brings stress – it impairs or strengthens families.
- Response to trauma matters – it crushes or grows you.
- Stubbornness is bad – perseverance is good.
- Imposing decisions – then repressing feedback is bad.
- Reconciliation is sweet – but often is delayed or denied.
- Delaying or denying reconciliation – is bad.

- Love is a beautiful thing – it trumps trauma.
- God advocates reconciliation – it restores love.
- I loved my family – imperfections did not stop that.
- Family love is good – foster it.

Career:

- The Great Depression was hard – it crushed our careers.
- My parents were farmers – without a farm.
- The Great Depression was very painful – it likely amplified stubbornness.
- Stubbornness with God (no church) – is a bad mistake.
- That "no church" breach – likely increased my father's drinking.

Lynn and Dorothy (Felton) Rogers side

God:

- The Rogers also left their church – when it became liberal.
- They came to our small church – but left because of its "add ons."
- Later, I went to my cousins' church – Grayton Rd. Baptist.
- All of the Felton/Rogers family members attended church regularly – all received salvation.

Family:

- Lynn Rogers Sr. died at age 43 – death is traumatic.
- Aunt Dorothy became a "widow" – being a "wife" was much easier.
- Five kids became fatherless – the eldest male became "father" at age 16.

- My mother rushed to help – these two sisters led together.
- My grandfather had a stroke – strokes paralyze.
- Paralytics require bedside care – aunts and cousins provided in-home care.
- Depression/death/stroke is hard – but we grew.
- The family closed ranks – forged by the two aunts.
- They simply expanded FAMILY – it was the right choice.
- All of us rose up and worked – We became COUSINS.
- I was learning family – a LOVE-CORED FAMILY.
- I brought that learning forward – into my marriage.

Career:

- All of us worked - we learned work ethics from our parents and grandparents.
- Our work ethic wasn't just sweat - it was Christian ethics.
- None of us COUSINS exploited or took advantage of customers – it violated our ethics.
- Bob and Lynn Jr. landscaped – to pay for seminary.
- They hired me – and mentored me into such ethics.
- Such ethics were in our parents – but now they are in the COUSINS.
- The COUSINS brought ethics forward – to all seven of our spouses.
- My wife-to-be shared these ethics – what a gift from God.
- We were NOT perfect – but we knew career ethics.
- COUSIN collaboration was strong – because it was love based.

Bob and Mary (Grose) Ewing side

God:

- They were occasional church attendees – of an Enlightened Protestant church.
- Their church became "enlightened" – just prior to this era.
- The Bible was seen to have errors – not the inspired word of God.
- Keith's church experience was ADDITIONS – Sally's was SUBTRACTIONS.
- Sally was hearing "Be good/not bad" – so she obeyed.
- Sally was learning ethics – but not salvation.

Family:

- The move from McComb to Cleveland – left family behind.
- So Sally's family of four – became a bonded Ewing family.
- Sally's love for her brother was strong – but 10 years is a culture gap.
- Bob's work was intense – Four of five diners were lost. Retaining the fifth was hard.
- Trauma and intense work – led Bob to a one-year mental breakdown.
- Sally's mother shielded Sally from trauma – Shirley Temple example.
- Sally's brother departed for war – just as the war ended.

Career:

- Accountant and teacher – became restaurant entrepreneurs.

- Four of five diners were lost to Great Depression – fifth requires workaholism.
- Father's extensive hours – required naps at home and in the restaurant.
- Mother "mothers" her two children – lovingly.
- Mother, son and Sally would soon join this work pattern.
- All four will close ranks – when they start over at the end of the war.
- The fifth diner will be replaced – by the Penguin Ice Cream store.
- Wow, Sally and her family – are bonded together by work.
- Lesson – food entrepreneurs work long hours.

As you have read about those stressful situations, it would be easy to conclude that God, Family and Career all had bad times: useless and harmful within the real world. NOT SO; losing our house, finding salvation but with baggage, experiencing the hazards of stubbornness, and having my parents separate were simply the refining environment in which God was shaping my life. I loved my grandfather, my father, my mother and Mrs. Wildy and that love was not breached by these Great Depression and War experiences. God was discipling me into a person:

Who could stand up to problems; not run away.
Who would hone his faith; salvation without the baggage.

Who would not be stubborn; it's too painful.

Who would ask, listen and use feedback; because each person has wisdom.

Who would seek God's guidance; and then obey Him.

I will validate this claim that these five people gains in my behavior were more important than the Great Depression property losses by taking you forward to an event 50 years later. We were having a very important President's Meeting in Alcoa. All of our business unit presidents were present, and we were working on a contentious problem with our CEO at the podium. We were divided and becoming angry with each other, whereupon the CEO stepped down and called me to the podium. He said to the presidents, "You are very fortunate that Keith is now going to take over this meeting instead of me, HE IS A NICE MAN." We resolved the issues amicably and favorably in 45 minutes. God molded me throughout my life to bring His ethics and ways to a corporate board room as an Executive Vice President.

Please bear with me as I am too humble to write that paragraph easily. But it is the truth, and for some reason, God arranged since kindergarten for me to one day bring His perspectives into Alcoa for a season. I was His ambassador that day at the podium, and many others.

* * *

Child to Adult: 1945 to 1957

The year 1945 was a tipping point for the world and for America. World War II ended on September 2, 1945. We celebrated with great joy that our troops and family members would now come home. Yet, on the day of celebration, our live-in tenant Frank McLane said, "The next war will be with Russia." I was stunned, shocked and overwhelmed to even imagine another war.

But Frank was right. Russia's losses during World War II – 26 million people of the total 52 million deaths – led to the Cold War, a period during which the United States and Russia built atomic bombs and then the more lethal hydrogen bomb in large numbers. Our joy at the end of World War II was cut short by more global conflict. As a ten-year-old boy, I experienced great fear that the bombing of Pearl Harbor would be repeated, with Russia as the enemy this time. A tense showdown in Cuba between our countries ended in withdrawal in 1962, but I still remember our deep emotions during that time.

Another important context to include is the status of our culture. The war effort had transitioned us out of the constrained living conditions within the decade-long Great Depression. By the end of the war, we became the intensely active, strongest industrial economy in the world! Our factories that had built cars before the war, then tanks, airplanes and military trucks during the war, converted back to cars. Our families (the Turnbulls and the Ewings) brought forward our workaholic predispositions into that burgeoning economy.

Also, in 1945, both Sally and I have NO, I repeat myself, NO comprehension of the evil of segregation that was the cultural norm of our nation and our city, Cleveland. We lived 10 miles west of the center of Cleveland and there were no African Americans in those 10 miles and the next 10 miles west. The only exception was a tiny cluster of about 10 railroad conductors who lived next to their railroad station about seven miles from where we lived. The African American community that did exist lived in ghetto-like circumstances to the east of Cleveland, where we rarely went. And, sad to say, nothing much had changed by the end of this 1945 to 1957 period. African Americans served bravely and effectively in World War II and then were relegated back into ghettos when they returned from the war. God, please forgive us for this blatant evil to these, Your beloved people. Belatedly, we confess, repent, and seek total reconciliation.

2

Our Love Story

I started this book with the story of how I met Sally at a young age, but God planned a love story for us that was intentionally lengthy.

It is important to understand our post-war culture as we discuss dating since this time period is prior to the "sexual revolution" of the mid-1970s. When Sally and I were teenagers, magazines and movies had no partial or total nudity. Strict movie censorship would not even permit the portrayal of a man and woman to lie in bed together, even if clothed. Through our high school days, our school constrained boy/girl courtship while on campus with the strict rule "no bodily contact." A boy could not even hold hands in school with his girlfriend. If there were any drugs being used amongst my schoolmates, I never saw it or was aware of it. None of my friends even discussed using drugs. Yet, most teens yearned for the day they could begin drinking alcohol. A 3.2% beer was legal at age 16 so a nearby bar sold only that weaker beer to cater to their "growing up" customers. I was the only one to avoid alcohol amongst my friends, except perhaps Kent Dean. Sally and I were one year apart in our school classes of 137 and 139 students and each class at graduation had only one pregnancy before graduation.

Another context to understand is there were no cell phones, internet, Facebook, etc. that these days give us perpetual communication. We had telephones for local calls, but long-distance calls were too expensive. We simply could not afford to use them for calls even to cities as close as Cleveland and Detroit. These constraints profoundly impact this portion of our Love Story.

Preteen Love Blossoms: Ages 11 and 12

In the years before Sally and I met, I "liked" a girl from church named Shirley Shirley (yes – her real name) and later became a "friend" of Roberta Turner. For preteens like us, "friend" meant that we played sports together, usually with my friends Jim Kemp and Nancy Jones.

When Roberta learned that I didn't know how to dance, she told me that was unacceptable for a boy-girl relationship. So she took me to her apartment and had me practice with her mother until I learned to dance. But Roberta later moved away.

It was only 20 miles but that was far enough that we ceased being a part of each other's lives.

Sally also had neighbors who she "liked" as her playmates and who later became her "friends," particularly twins Stanley and Stephen Atkinson. They played together and even were sick with whooping cough together, which allowed them to play table games in Sally's basement as they recovered. Stanley was 10 and Sally was 11; active children having a good time playing together. She recorded her feelings in one of the journals that she wrote in every day for a decade.

Then the Atkinson boys moved away from Cleveland to Detroit. However, Stan and Sally did not cease being part of each other's lives the way Roberta and I had done. In January of 1947, Sally's journal entry shows them as normal pre-teen children. But by the time the twins moved away twelve months later, Sally and Stan had begun to speak about love and to draw pictures of hearts with each other's names inside. Preteen love had blossomed so that Stan and Sally chose to continue their love, even though Stan moved 170 miles away from Sally.

Letters Replace Seeing – A Letter Each Month for Two Years

At ages 11 and 12, they had locked into a love commitment that was almost impossible to sustain. Pre-teen is the early stage of love and is sometimes called puppy love. But now they had no way to grow their love via the normal ways like embracing, dancing, kissing, talking, laughing, crying or even seeing. Their only way to grow was via written letters. Pay close attention to this insight; letters are NOT the primary language of love. The seven I have just listed, as well as others, are precursors to intercourse. Letters are merely an analog, a model, and a conveyor in written words of the feelings that two lovers try to experience on a sheet of paper.

Sally and Stan were both diligent in their letter writing for two years at about a letter per month. But then both began experiencing the physical elements of love with others. Sally was taught to dance (a school requirement) and then danced with Gene LeFavour at a school dance for newly taught dancers. Stan began dancing several months earlier. Both were experiencing slightly the "touches" of love with local partners while writing about their love for each other in letters. Both of them tried very hard for two years, and Sally (amazingly) for 5 1/2 years as Stan was the teenager she loved.

Keith and Sally Date – My First Date/Her First Date

I knew none of this background when I asked Sally for a date on February 3, 1951 when we were in 9th and 10th grades. It was two years after Stan's move, and I had unknowingly walked into their story.

Sally and Keith dating

I was nervous as I had never asked a girl for a date, nor had she ever been asked to go on a date. But she said yes, and our lives were forever changed. I opened the door for her to move past her pre-teen experience with the emotion of love that she and Stan had barely begun before he moved away. I became the way in which Sally could add dating, dancing, and holding hands with a boy with whom she could see, talk to, and laugh with. Because of her love for Stan, she had set very tight boundaries for herself that she absolutely would not cross, like never kiss and never go steady with anyone else.

Stan Stops Letters – Total Silence for 20 Months

However, three weeks prior to our date together, she received a letter from Stan asking;

> *"Sally there is something bothering me. Will you say yes or no and be sincere too. Up at camp I heard that (from John Davis) you like some other kid at your High School. Is it true?"*

Sally immediately wrote back. I do not know what she replied, but I do know that our date could not have been the cause of Stan's questions. Why? Because I had not even asked her for a date until three weeks after his letter. What I do know is that Stan stopped writing letters: no communication whatsoever for 20 months.

Stan Explains His Silence – "It's time for us to quit."

Then he wrote a single letter dated October 2, 1952 that stated:

> *Dear Sally,*
>
> *I will tell you what I have done in the past two years. The last letter you got from me was in February 1951... If you really must know, I did like you very much, but I soon realised that we could be nothing to each other except just friends. Another thing is that*

the grade, age and location would keep us apart. So you stop thinking that we both like each other ... Now I hope that we can just be friends to each other. When I stopped writing, it was when I was just going into high school in Detroit. ... Hope we can both be friends.

Your friend,

Stan Atkinson

P.S. If you would have been my age, in the same grade and gone to the same school. Then we could have made out with each other in every way.

Sally Reacts to Stan's Letter – Tears and "He's probably right."

Sally cried over his letter because she liked him so much but thought "he is probably right." She then immediately wrote him back and then wrote in her journal,

"When I got home, I found a letter to me from Stan- the first one since Feb of 1951. He told me what I'd been trying to deny all these 3 ½ years. – Since we were separated, we should break up and just be good friends. I wrote him back right away."

Note that she ends with the word "probably." She has just gone through 20 months of no letters from Stan and then a letter saying, "It's over." Even still, she couldn't release herself from her love commitment for Stan that she made at age 12. Her journal entries continued to declare her love for him even after his breakup letter. Thereafter, there was another drought of letters for six months.

They See Each Other Six Months Later – Try a Restart

Then, Sally saw Stan for only the second time since he moved away four years earlier.

Stan, Sally and twin brother Steve

His family of five came for a 24-hour visit during which there was no private time for Sally and Stan to talk. But it restarted the exchange of letters for them to attempt to reignite their love. Both were excited for a month, but after two months, Stan reflected:

"There is one letter out of many that made me think a little, it was the one that said that we never have been to a date to a dance or ever seen each other more than once a year. What love did we experience together all these years anyway, maybe it is our love for each other more than anything else. What do you think it is?"

Then two weeks later he wrote:

"This Keith Turnbull must be crazy about you the way you say that he has been trying for 3 years. But that's the way some boys and girls are."

Then there was a gradual cool down for two months as Sally invited Stan to visit any time during the summer and he turned her down as too busy and he then informed her that he was moving to California. Sally cried, then silence. Stan began his third period of zero letters, this time for nine months. Then on April 1, 1954, he sent his final letter.

April 1, 1954

Dear Sally,

I am sending this letter to let you know about the request that I received from you not too long ago. I believe you had asked me about going to your Senior Class Dance in the early part of June, if I am not mistaken it was June 4, 5, & 6th. I am sorry to say that I can-not come merely because of the activities here in Detroit. I am sure that there are many boys who would be very happy to go to a Senior Class Dance. Especially being asked by a very noted senior such as your self at your Senior High. I thank you very much for asking me though and appreciate you thinking of me. I hope that you have lots of fun through your senior year and at the college in Florida where you plan to go.

Yours truly,

Stan Atkinson

Tears of Loss and Release - Her Preteen Love was not to be her Lifelong Love

Sally's Journal Entry

Thursday, April 1, 1954

Today I had my French and history exams. After school, I took Ellis home. (This morning I worked on announcing over the P.A.; 2nd period I defeated Heinzerling and then Rehor in badminton singles.) <u>After I got home from school, I found a letter from Stan — a very stiff and formal refusal to the senior prom with me. I know he doesn't like me now!</u> I painted 2 signs for the Penguin, did some English and watched TV. Got to bed at 11:00. Cold.

Sally cried and these tears were both for loss and release. She had been faithful beyond measure to the pre-teen commitment she made to Stan. Why had she persisted? She had to; because she is a very caring, principled, and committed person. She made a love agreement when she was 12 years old and felt called to honorably carry it out. The fact that she couldn't mature from her pre-teen love normally did not release her from her agreement to love. So she persevered for growth without embracing, dancing, kissing, seeing, touching, hearing, laughing or crying with Stan. Those were simply the impairments to growth that she had accepted. When she was 14 and I asked her to go on a date to a movie, she said yes such that she could experience the most preliminary aspects of boy/girl relationships such as seeing, hearing and laughing, while barely moving forward to touching. Attending a movie was fine but touching was limited to holding hands. With a date to a movie, parent driver to and from, she moved past her insular world of "letters only." She had already drawn up her strict boundary rules of no kissing and no going steady so that such a date would not intrude into her love for Stan.

Finally, Sally was able to sever the love promise she had made to Stan 5 1/2 years earlier. Only with such a closure could she make peace within herself that she had honorably respected Stan.

Amazingly, as soon as she severed the Stan connection, she fell in love with me. I had been pushed out of her life a year earlier and had not had any contact with her for nine months. Then I bought an ice cream cone from her at her parents' ice cream store and was instantly bonded forever to my wife of 63 years.

Read how Sally described it in her journal:

Sunday, April 4, 1954
94th Day—271 days to follow

☑ CLEAR
☐ CLOUDY
☐ RAIN
☐ SNOW

This morning I awoke at 11:30. I messed around til after lunch; then studied English all afternoon. From 5:15 — 8:00 I worked up at the Penguin. Gretch dropped in to see the place & say "hi". Also, Keith came up — on a cane. He was with Jimmy Kemp, & Kemp was driving his father's '54 Cadillac. Anyway, they had an accident, & Keith is on a cane — hurt in his leg. I got no details on how it all happened. After seeing him, I've fallen in love with him again. I guess I just wasn't "mature" enough to want his love before, but I think that now I do. ♡ Keith ♡ I felt so sorry for him on that cane; he looked so sad. I studied his. & Eng. until 9:30. Then watched TV til 10:30. Cool out, but we were real busy at the Penguin.

Trust me as I tell you why and how this happened. It was God, all God. He was guiding us, teaching us and giving both of us persistence beyond reason and hearts of kindness for our assignments that He would soon entrust to us, individually, as a family and in our careers. So, of course, He would join us in a single day, and, of course, His joining of us would penetrate our hearts so deeply that we would be utterly inseparable. Of course, this was an extension of the shaping God had been doing to each of us during the Great Depression and War.

His joining of us would penetrate our hearts so deeply that we would be utterly inseparable.

You now may be wondering what I was doing during these years that I have described about Sally. Well, first of all, I knew nothing about Stan and this 5 ½-year effort Sally and he had to sustain their pre-teen love. Then secondly, I never wrote a journal as Sally did, so I cannot be as accurate in my description.

I did know that I didn't do well at first when I chose ditching her sled as a way to get acquainted when she was 14 years old and I was 15. But I was thrilled when both of us had the first date that either of us ever had and we did it by going to a movie. Thereafter we both liked ice skating together. It was really nice to hold hands. By the time we had made those gains, I knew that Sally was an uncommonly kind and loving person, and also really fun to be around.

However, the boundaries she had set, and the way she adhered to them, meant I could never contemplate marriage during those three years. I could not even ask her to go steady because I could tell she would say "no." No kissing prevailed for two years as a restraint. However, I eventually innovated my way past that barrier by kissing her on her forehead and then eventually on her lips. But by that time, she was beginning to move me out of her life so that she could date other boys.

In the Bible, Moses led his people out of slavery in Egypt, but they became stalled in the Wilderness for 40 years. During their trip out of Egypt, the Israelites reached the Red Sea and had no way to cross, so God parted the sea and they walked across. Our first three years of dating felt to me like I was Moses wandering around in the Wilderness.

Toward the end of the third year of dating in high school, there was a stark shift downward in my standing with her. She did not want to see me or interact with me at all. It was absolute separation when I graduated from high school. I am one year older, so I was soon to be a freshman in engineering, and she would soon begin her senior year of high school. At that time, a boy I will call John Doe became her boyfriend and he was very different than her ethics construct. They would interact a lot in school each day and go on dates. She was trying to love him. But she would keep running into the fact that they were opposites in many ways, but she kept trying anyway. She dated a lot of other boyfriends in that time period. I believe God planted John Doe into her life to give her a good insight into mismatching. Then, she began dating Kent Dean, my close friend since kindergarten, whose ethics were more similar to hers.

Meanwhile, I too dated several other girls in college until I met Jane Doe. She was very attractive, we had dates, and we got along well. She was quite anxious to go steady, and after three years of not being able to go steady with Sally, I agreed to go steady with Jane Doe. I then learned that we had very different goals and views on life. Shortly after we began to go steady, she was anxious to move forward into intercourse and I was surprised. That highway wasn't one I wanted to travel before marriage.

That's the God trail of puberty management God had for Sally and me. It was stark, amazing and beautiful. That's where we were when God decided it was time for his miraculous intervention. After ten months of total separation and three years of wandering, He used an ice cream cone to seal our love for each other. She and I had zero contemplation of marriage until I bought that chocolate chip ice cream cone in April 1954. Then, before the month ended, we were planning our marriage. Like Moses before us, the Red Sea had parted in a single day. Sally and I wandered for three years, then the sea parted and we were in love in one day.

When I went back and read those journal entry pages, I had not even been mentioned in her journal for many months, and then, all of a sudden she's in love with me. She saw me walking a few days after the ice cream cone and offered me a ride. We took a second look at each other and began to realize that something was starkly different. We started testing it by asking and talking. Within a few days, we were both aware that a profound thing had happened; I love her and she loves me.

Sally and I had some "housekeeping" to do that took about three weeks. She had two dates with Kent Dean already set up, so she had to back out of those gracefully. Since I had been going steady with Jane Doe, I had to cancel our date to her senior prom, stop going steady and explain that it's over. Within less than two weeks, Sally and I had a heart-to-heart talk and I revealed everything about Jane Doe's failed seduction intent. Friend Kent Dean became a broker for the two of us. Kent came to me and told me he'd been dating Sally frequently, but now I better take Sally seriously because she was now deeply in love with me. He told me, "You need to step up and follow through with what Sally wants because she has totally written me off. The wonderful situation that you're now in is love and she has cast aside all other boys." I took his advice and Sally and I spoke with full candor in long conversations in my truck. Total honesty with each other was established within our love for each other. On May 8, we exchanged her high school class ring and my Campus Club pin (similar to a fraternity pin), declaring that we are going steady.

We've chosen each other and now look forward to marriage and children. However, her parents perceive me to be from "the wrong side of the tracks." When I picked Sally up for dates in my old pickup truck, her parents sensed that our dating might eventually lead to marriage and worried that their daughter would be poor. They let her ride in the tired old truck but insisted thereafter that she must go to college so she could support herself. Therefore, Sally must graduate from college if she decides to marry me because I am a pauper.

We love each other and we are through our first month of reconciliation of all past matters. However, we have to hunker down to the reality of this four-year separation looming ahead of us because she must go to college. It was April of her senior year of high school so we had one summer together but then she would go off to college at Miami University in Oxford, Ohio, which is six hours away. The next stage was God governing and nurturing our love and securing Sally's relationship with God because she was not a believer yet.

Consequences:

1. Courtship - including morals of abstinence from drugs, alcohol, smoking and intercourse.
2. Sally's faith - she was now moving on a pathway to salvation.

3. Marriage anticipation – upon a foundation of unconditional love.
4. Keith's faith - baggage was gone.
5. Parenting - yearning to marry and to build our family.

We believe that we had a God-orchestrated courtship of patience/love/marriage. He arranged for Sally to have uncommonly safe ethics. When Sally was young, her father sat her down, and had her drink liquor. She decided it tasted bad and threw up. He then had her smoke a cigarette, which caused her to cough and wheeze. His message was that these vices were addictive, and though he did them, he did not want her to ever start.

In contrast, my father didn't sit down and talk to me directly about alcohol or smoking. He drank liquor on occasion, about once a month or so. He'd get drunk, take a drive and have an accident, repeatedly, which led to his firing from the company where he had worked for about 20 years. My brother told me that alcoholism can be hereditary, and he had decided to never find out if he had such an addiction. I decided to do the same.

I also received mentoring from Dr. Dean, whose son Kent was my best friend since kindergarten. I noticed a lot of Pepsi-Cola bottles in their kitchen and asked what they were all about. Dr. Dean said he had previously smoked. When he did surgery on people who smoked, he saw their lungs and was horrified by how they were black and deteriorated. Therefore, every time he wanted a cigarette, he drank a Pepsi. I resolved to never smoke. Before we even met, Sally and I had decided we would follow a highway that didn't involve either vices.

Sally and I were getting to know each other better in anticipation of marriage and children, but we both were resolved to virginity. We could have deeper friendship but no intercourse. During the Great Depression and War, I learned through COUSINS that love is precious. Then, as the tagalong, I watched as my cousins and brother fell in love and married before me. They knew God designed marriage and designated intercourse as a beautiful expression of marital love. It was a God principle that Sally and I embraced.

We believe that our courtship was unusual enough that we should share this portion of our life with you in detail. The journal entries Sally wrote every day for eight years would be worth reading as a memoir because it is so authentic. But it is mostly important for you because what we have shared is a vivid description of how God mentors us. You and we are each a product of God's love and, to an extent, a captive of our culture. Your life story will be different than mine. But God yearns to travel with you regardless of how you have lived so far. Read on. Our entire life story is a love story.

We understand that you are in a vastly different culture than we were in 70 years ago. Do not stop reading because of that difference. You will find that most of our God/Family/Career experiences are applicable to the life story you are living, no matter your life experience or journey.

3

Sally's Salvation

Sally and I had an instantaneous deep love, and we knew
each other well, but we now were really getting to know each
other in our four years of waiting for marriage during Sally's
college years. We learned to collaboratively make decisions,
even the hard ones, and how to not fight. It was a progressive
weaving together during these college years. But surprisingly,
I was not pressuring her about her faith in God. It was a carry
forward from my childhood days when I tried evangelizing
childhood friends with my salvation plus baggage and was
teased and physically abused. Concurrently, Sally retained the
"Enlightened Protestant" faith from her childhood and
upbringing. The God who gifted us with love in a single day
was now going to take us through a long process to merge our
faiths just in time for our marriage. What an awesome God!

Sally's church had an omission of the salvation message

that my church held precious: she was in a church that did not emphasize salvation. It was a liberal Protestant church that she did not attend often. They taught her to be good and not bad. But the fact that she was not saved, and needed to be, was in the hands of the Lord. The path God chose for her was a professor in a religion class in her last semester of college.

When Sally went away to college, we stopped officially going steady. We were so deeply in love that we were certain that we would not impair our bond by giving each other the right to date others so that each of us could participate in college social life. We had dates with other people but wrote love letters to each other every day. I never wavered and she never wavered. We solved our lonesomeness problem by my going back and forth from Cleveland to Miami University in Oxford, OH, sometimes by hitchhiking nine hours each way. Sally was always my number one.

Then her classmate Bill McFarland came along in Sally's senior year of college and he was different from others she dated previously because they were together longer and more frequently. They would play tennis and do homework together, sometimes three contacts per day. She told him from the beginning that he can date her, but she can never love him. He had never kissed a girl and did not kiss Sally. Then they took the same religion course and met together to study for it. Both of their church backgrounds were the enlightened Protestant church. God arranged for her studying with Bill and the teaching of their professor to lead Sally to salvation.

Sally skillfully recorded (without personal comment) the material that the professor taught. It was the method that had served her well as she attained her high grades, always above the 3.5/4.0 threshold. Miami University had set that threshold as their requirement for her to increase her class load each semester from 15 to 21 credits, the number that would let her graduate in three years instead of four. Our marriage is now an entire year earlier than we had expected. She kept her class notes for 63 years and we read them to use in this life story.

Her professor began with "What is religion," then moved into the broad concept of God from a Judeo-Christian perspective. He ignored Islam, Buddhism, etc. as he focused upon Christianity and its range of beliefs. He accurately described the enlightened theology of Sally's type of church and the conservative theology of my church. As Sally and I read her notes, we were amazed at the clarity and accuracy of the professor's teachings. When he got about a quarter of the way through the course, he superbly described the message I had heard from Mrs. Wildy more than a decade earlier, but without any of the excess baggage that I had received. Shortly after that, Sally's notes changed from passive (just recording what the professor said) to discerning (adding what she was catching onto). Her writings thereafter moved from discerning to believing ("I know this particular point and I believe it"). Then, as the semester was near its end, the professor again presented, and with sharp clarity, the salvation message in Sally's notes. This time, she owned it. Her notes (10 pages long) expressed her faith in Jesus Christ as her Savior. Her college professor for a class called "religion" was in fact an evangelist who, over a four-month period, bonded my fiancée and me into a tightly shared faith in Christ. It took Sally one day to fall in love with me and a four-month exposition by an evangelist to fall in love with God. We were married one week after our college graduations.

As Sally and I read her religion course notes to write this book, we became curious about Bill and called him. He had stayed with his Protestant theology, earned a PhD in economics, and worked in that field for 20 years. Then he went to seminary and became a Protestant pastor for 20 years.

Our love story consists of early dating, then a period of no traction dating, and then the implanting of other people to date into our lives, which had given us a season of learning things to embrace and things to avoid. We then had an instantaneous switch, which replaced rejection with deep love. It has never thereafter occurred to me to love anyone other than Sally in the 63 years we have been married. I have had an entire lifetime with absolute certainty that this is my mate. It has been God's intent for us to have total confidence in each other. It isn't just that we took one step to arrive at marriage. We were prepared over a long period of time. Now, as we next celebrate our marriage, God told us that we can experience the forever, unconditional love He had always intended for us.

4

Marriage – Finally and Forever

Our long-awaited wedding was on June 15, 1957 – one week after we graduated from college. We were anxious to get married. Our marriage ceremony was conducted by my two cousins Bob Rogers and Lynn Rogers, both of whom were now pastors. The ceremony was loving, bonding, mentoring and completely designed from the marriage God prescribes in the Bible. Bob Rogers led the service as he spoke it, prayed, and guided our activities such as the exchanging of rings. Lynn Rogers sang messages of love for each other and love for God.

One song used verses from Ruth 1:16 in the Bible that Bob spoke as follows: "Entreat me not to leave thee, or to return from following after thee, for whither thou goest, I will go, and where thou lodgest, I will lodge, thy people shall be my people, and thy God my God."

The other three songs were popular songs of the era that were selected by Lynn Rogers to represent a threesome: God/Sally/Keith. Then he only sang the part of each song that conveyed God/wife/husband bonding.

Notice the God words in the song *Walk Hand in Hand With Me* - "Eternity, Faith, Believe in Me, Lift your head up high and Destiny."

Walk hand in hand with me through all eternity
Have faith, believe in me, give me your hand
Love is a symphony of perfect harmony
When Lovers such as we walk hand in hand

Be not afraid, for I am with you all the while
So lift your head up high and look toward the sky

Walk hand in hand with me, this is our destiny
No greater love could be, walk hand in hand
Walk with me

In the next song *I Love You Truly*, I held one of Sally's hands and God held the other. Lynn stopped midway through the first song and immediately connected it to the part of the second song that sealed the depth of the love we share and the security it imparts during times of sorrow:

I love you truly, truly dear
Life with its sorrow, life with its tears
Fades into dreams when I feel you are near
For I love you truly, truly dear.

Ah love, 'tis something to feel your kind hand
Ah yes, 'tis something by your side to stand
Gone is the sorrow, gone doubt and fear
For you love me truly, truly dear.

Then, later in the service, Lynn sang the part of the *Lord's Prayer* that commissions us to live out our marriage in conformance to God's kingdom here on earth.

Our Father
Which art in heaven
Hallowed be thy name
Thy kingdom come
Thy will be done
On earth
As it is in heaven.

It was so very precious to us that they used these carefully selected portions of four songs to convey God's messages to us. "Wither thou goest, I will go" was a favorite song of ours at that time. I've included the written words of each song in this book so that you can see the foundation that my two cousins built into our marriage.

We suggest that you now "attend" our wedding in written text and pictures. We recorded all the words of the wedding in an old-fashioned reel-to-reel tape recorder and transcribed some of the key themes to share with you now.

You will see the close relation of the words with the Biblical descriptions of God's design for marriage. They are not routine repetitions. They are instead a road map that God designed as the pathway to the loving marriage He intends for us to have. I have selected some portions to share with you now so that you will understand why Sally and I rushed back to the entire marriage content when we chose to take our marriage experience to the high side several weeks later.

I promise you that we believe every single word that you will next read, and we tried (though imperfectly) to live them out for all 63 years of our marriage. You are reading key elements of a covenant that we made with God. May your reading of it touch your heart.

We are gathered together to join this man and this woman in holy matrimony. It is an honorable estate instituted by God, and signifying the mystical union between Christ and His church. Therefore, do not enter into it inadvisably but reverently, discretely, and in the fear of God. Remember that love and love alone will avail as the foundation of a happy home. If you keep your vows and do the will of your Heavenly Father, your life will be

full of joy and a home which you are establishing will abide in peace. Keith, wilt thou have this woman to be your wedded wife, to live together in the holy estate of matrimony, wilt thou love her, comfort her, honor and keep her in sickness and in health and forsaking all others keep thee only unto her so long as you both shall live. (Keith – I will.) Then Sally vowed this to Keith.

Who giveth this woman to be married to this man? (Bob Ewing – Her mother and I do.)

Do you Keith Turnbull take Sally Ewing whom you now hold by your hand as your true and lawful wife and, God helping you, will you love, cherish, honor and protect her, cleaving only unto her until God by death shall separate you? (Keith – I do.) Then Sally vowed the same but "protect" was replaced with "obey."

We exchanged rings as tokens of our love, emblems of eternity, imperishable faith and union unto death. Then we declared: "Entreat me not to leave thee or to return from following after thee, for whither thou goest I will go, and where thou lodgest I will lodge, thy people shall be my people and thy God my God."

Then we were pronounced to be as husband and wife in the name of the Father, the Son, and the Holy Spirit. Amen.

The commissioning prayer included: Thank you our Lord and Heavenly Father. We pray that thou will use their lives that they might be a witness of thyself. May they have peace of heart, resting upon the assurance that Jesus is their guide. We pray that these two united together in holy wedlock with thy blessing may go through life searching out Thy will for their lives. We pray for these two. In Jesus' name, Amen.

Remember Keith, so love Sally in such a way that it will be easy for her to reverence and obey you. I now take pleasure in presenting to you, Mr. and Mrs. Keith Turnbull.

Read again that Bob Rogers closed our wedding with a reminder to me: "Remember Keith: so love Sally in such a way that it will be easy for her to reverence and obey you." I heard him clearly and have made that my lifelong intent.

God was the initiator of marriage in the book of Genesis and then describes its design, intent and behaviors clearly in Ephesians, Colossians and I Peter. Major features are:

- God is the designer of marriage.
- He encourages us that married love is like God's love.
- It is the greatest person-to-person love that we can attain.
- As husband, I am the head; God will help me to lead properly.
- I am not authorized to be a dictator, quite the opposite.
- My wife is to obey me as her husband, but then, because of our love,
- As her husband, I must make it "easy for her to obey."

- God will perpetually coach me on how to be "easy for her to obey."
- As husband, I must nurture and grow my wife into the fullness of the woman God intends her to be.
- And, as husband, I must persevere in "this fullness" role,
- Even if it means losing my life for her, like Jesus did for us.

  AND

- In all of the above, God is our perpetual traveling partner, guiding our steps and empowering us in our marital roles.

We have not lived perfectly in these roles that God prescribed for us, but they have been our guiding beacons for the 63 years we have been married. The closer we get to them, the sweeter our marriage becomes. We are both in love and loving, 63 years later.

***

Our honeymoon was spectacular, in our ways of defining that word. Finally, after seven years, we are together, just the two of us, which was all that really mattered. We drove around Michigan, seeing its beauty, staying in motels, renting a boat and catching turtles. But most of all, we enjoyed being together from then to forever.

There were a few glitches during the trip but none of them mattered: We were too much in love to care. We didn't have much money so we asked Sally's parents to give us their old Buick. They said no: it is too old and unreliable. We pleaded "Please, it's that car or no car" so they relented.

Sally's parents with the Buick

We intended to drive to Toledo the first night after our wedding, but once there, the lodgings were all full due to a huge golf tournament in town. So we drove further into the night, finally finding a motel in Michigan at 3 am. The next day, we rented a boat, caught turtles, and got severe sun burns - not too wise for honeymooners. The following day, the Buick overheated, so we spent part of that day at an auto repair garage. As we traveled farther north into Michigan, we hiked into a beautiful forest only to discover that it was the mosquito capital of the state. On the way home, our Buick ceased running while we were on the Ohio Turnpike. After sitting for about an hour, a repairman came and fixed it in five minutes. Our groomsman Cy Bliss had tuned the engine just before our wedding and hadn't tightened a bolt on the distributor points quite tightly enough. We then drove in the fixed car.

Yet, I repeat, our honeymoon was spectacular. None of those glitches mattered. We didn't worry, get frustrated or feel sad. Nuts with the bothersome car. We're finally together, and overheating, sunburn, mosquitoes and distributor points were trivial; mere nuisances within our life story. We were nestled within the worldview Bob and Lynn had just prayed us into and we basked in that as we waited for the repairman to fix our car. Spectacular indeed!

Writing this chapter brings tears of joy to me. How thankful Sally and I are that God gifted us with marriage and then travelled with us these 63 years. Our learning lesson is just one: If you marry, choose to have God as your constant companion.

5

Careers - 1945 to 1957

Concurrently with this love story that led to marriage, Sally and I grew into the careers that we would pursue after marriage. When the war ended in 1945, Sally was nine and I was ten years old and both of us had family chores, both inside and outside our homes. Then, as you read earlier in the first chapter, both of us delivered newspapers as our first paying jobs at one penny per paper.

Sally's Career

Sally's career broadened when her brother returned from the army in 1947 and joined his father in launching and operating the Ewing's Penguin, a high-quality ice cream store. It became an all-family, all-consuming successful business: 12 hours a day, 7 days a week for the entire ice cream season – closed only for the cold winter months. Sally began to work there before she reached the age of 16 when she could legally work the window selling to customers so she worked in the back room where ice cream was made: processing the fresh fruits they would use in their ice cream, cleaning, doing inventory, etc. The ice cream was excellent, the ethics impeccable, and her father greeted every customer with a big smile (whether he was having a good day or not). Sally was being mentored in an excellent family-owned workplace in which her father had carried forward his diner workaholic methods, from diner meals into ice cream treats.

Sally's brother Bill and her father began this business by spending hours with hand counters to see which intersections were busiest and would be the best place to build their business. The result: the corner of Center Ridge Road, one business away from Wagar Road in Fairview Park, next to Rocky River. The corner shop was an open market selling fruits and vegetables, and a shopping mall went in later on the kitty-corner side of that intersection. They proceeded with building an ice cream stand called "The Penguin," which provided work for them, Sally's mother, another counter girl later, and several young men who drove the one ice cream truck and five pedal bicycle carts through the local streets. The business thrived.

Sally with a Penguin cart

Sally fell in love with me one day without even pausing in her work when I came to the Penguin to buy an ice cream cone in 1954. However, in the months following that, our dates had to be from 11 pm to 1 am because she did not finish work until that time, seven days a week. Her father taught her the business by having her count money and put the coins in their paper tubes. Her journal entries recorded the earnings of each day and often a comment on how well the business was going. She was paid the going wage for a server and put virtually all of it into a savings account. She became twice business savvy: at Miami University where she majored in business, and in the real-life Penguin business where she could learn by doing with her skilled and loving father as her mentor. Through high school, college and into our marriage, Sally continued to work at the Penguin. Six months after our first son Ken was born, she strapped him onto a seat on the back of her bike and rode him the three miles from our home to the Penguin so she could do the morning preparations there.

Services at the Protestant church were usually squeezed out by the perpetually open sign on the Penguin (11 am to 11 pm). Winter was a respite from work when attendance at her Protestant church was attainable. But most winters, they went to Florida to vacation for two to four weeks.

Sally also had a volunteer "career" during high school that was extensive and broad: from athletics to service organizations to school office typing, often in a leadership role. Sally's career from 1945 to 1957 was focused with continuous work in Penguin business, very little church career and very diverse high school work and mentoring.

Keith's Career

Sally and I both worked hard on our jobs during middle school, high school and college. I moved from job to job through those years, trying to raise money for my tuition, dormitory and food. Sally's parents paid all of her college costs but my parents could not afford to pay any of mine. Sally's parents' concern that I was from the "wrong side of the tracks" was in fact true from this dollar perspective. Here is my list of disparate jobs (forgetting a dozen or so) and then commenting on them later:

- Three paper routes, not concurrently – 1 cent per paper
- Golf caddy, class B then A - $2-4 per day for B and $4-8 per day for A
- Greenhouse (inside) floor labor – 75 cents per hour
- Greenhouse builder, glazer and painter - $1 per hour
- Landscaper and tractor operator - $1 per hour
- Tractor booker/operator/collector - $1 per hour
- Flower deliverer – greenhouse to florist - $1 per hour
- Flower deliverer (florist to home) – per flowerpot or bouquet
- Envelope stuffer for yogurt ads - $1.00 per hour
- Chevrolet factory employee - $2 per hour
- Dog kennel cleaner (every morning and evening) - $1.25 per hour
- Pet store salesperson - $1.25 per hour
- Case Tech laborer - $1 per hour
- House to house deliverer of Tide detergent samples - $1 per hour
- Alcoa, summer intern - $2.50 per hour
- And more (about 15)

Despite my hard work, I earned enough money for my freshman year, but not enough for my sophomore and beyond. There were no school loan processes in place such as those that have become broadly and easily available in recent decades. However, some loan money was available from the Case Alumni Association. So I applied. They said they preferred not to lend money this early – when I was just entering my sophomore year. Their reason was that the pressure would be so high (courses plus money) that I would likely flunk out. I pleaded, they listened, and I got the loan. By my senior year, I was working 40 hours a week plus carrying a full 20 credits per semester school load.

I learned what jobs I did not want, which I will list with #1 being the worst and the following being next worse.

1. Stuffing envelopes – It was a brain-dead job that drove me bonkers. I started at 8 am and after an eternity, I'd think it must be time for lunch. Not so, it was only 8:50 am.
2. Bad boss – The first Case Tech job was fairly boring, and I had a boss who had made it forbidden to speak from 8 am to noon, and from 12:30 to 4:30.
3. Delivering Tide samples – It was winter, I passed them out by walking in a wealthy suburb, and no bathroom access.

Now switching to the best jobs:
1. Alcoa, by far: They gave me very interesting and challenging work to do, right in the field of my education. It was learn-by-doing. Then once a week, they brought all 20 interns together to teach us the scope of the business and how we would fit in. Only much later did I learn that this was their recruitment process, sorting out the interns who matched their business needs.
2. Landscaping and Tractor: I enjoyed working at Rogers Brothers Landscaping because it was a business started by

my two cousins to pay their way through seminary. We worked hard together; we had sharpened our collaboration during our COUSINS-bonding period. They, of course, were farmers with a tractor, highly skilled since their youth, and they mentored me into their competence.

3. Cleaning kennels: A choice that you likely will think odd. But the pet shop was next door to my apartment and the owners knew my need for money that I could earn every morning and every afternoon with no wasted time or travel cost. I did it for four years, even after I was married. The pet shop owner and I became great friends.

This eclectic set of work experiences earned me enough money to graduate with tolerable debt, inside the limits the Alumni Association had specified. I had learned how important it is to be in a two-way job; simultaneously valuable and interesting to both the employer and employee. I had a spattering of domain experience across a broad range of career choices. I also learned how important it was to serve your employer well and to do the best job you could.

I have chosen not to summarize the 1945 to 1957 era with a list of Learning Lessons like I wrote after the preceding era. I trust that the life story itself has been interesting, compelling and clear such that you can see and take away learnings for your life story. I have titled the next era (1957 to 1962) "Our Foundation: the convergence of **God** (shared faith), **Family** (married forever) and **Career** (God's calling). Our foundation became real. Dreams came true. You will see these leveraging each other in this next five years and thereafter, blowing past our earlier dreams into places we never believed possible. We have one more preparatory step: my MS and PhD at Case.

By now, you know that we have grown up Loving (God imparted), Working (Jobs done well), Collaborating (constructively together), Mentored and Mentoring (enhancing each other), Strengthened (through Great Depression and War), and Learners (eager for more) with shared Faith (followers of God). Some might see us as weak, not ready for the harshness of the REAL WORLD such as; the adversarial methods used in the United States Senate, too caring to lead an unfriendly takeover, not brazen enough to launch a war, or not selfish enough to exploit a weakened neighbor. Guilty as accused. Neither of us have the ethics for these.

We are the counter proposal that leads with kindness. Neither of us wanted or would have succeeded in adversarial roles. But both of us found roles that aligned with who we had become as we grew in our walk with God, married to launch our family and progressed in our careers. Those happenings begin in this next five years (1957 to 1962) and then continue to today in 2020.

We returned from our honeymoon to our home, our bed and our jobs. Well, it was sort of like that. A professor from Case was taking his family on an extended summer vacation, so he needed someone to house sit and care for his cats. I was well prepared for that role from my four-year job of cleaning kennels. His house was older and had a maid's room above the garage. So we slept in that room on the bed that was already there. Not elegant, but we were thrilled to be "at home" together.

The next day, we both went to work in our new jobs. Sally's job was as a secretary for a manager in the Glass Division of Diamond Alkali Company. She was a business major and graduated cum laude, but in those days, women rarely got jobs in business other than as a secretary. Her pay was $325 a month. By contrast, I had several job offers at $500 to $520 a month as a metallurgical engineer in steel, or nickel, or aluminum. I chose the aluminum path at Alcoa in Cleveland but only for the summer, such that I could return to Case and earn $320 a month while earning a master's degree.

6

Our Foundation – 1957 to 1962

Sally had always been a Ewing of the Ewing family and I had always been a Turnbull of the Turnbull family. After a seven-year wait through our dating years, we moved out of those two houses and began cohabitating. For three years, we both had harbored a dream of Marriage and Family. Both of those are much larger than cohabitating, and our marriage is now a week-old reality and, in a sense, so is our family. We do not yet have a child, but we are now a family of two. We go to work in the morning, come home and share evenings together. We could have just settled into those realities of "together in a house" as many newlyweds do. But we dared not to even pause there. God would not let us, and the carefully scripted wedding words of Bob and Lynn had imparted fresh visions of marriage vastly beyond our prior comprehension. So we began doing as God had directed.

Principle 1 - Leave and Cleave

We had become Mr. and Mrs. Turnbull. For sure. But beyond that, we had:

- Left our parents.
- Cleaved to one another.
- Become one flesh.
- Are now walking hand in hand with each other for eternity.

The sum of these parts is the high side of both marriage and family. High Side is a term that I've assigned to the extremely positive state that we have reached in our marriage. We had anxiously anticipated marriage for three years and had dreams about how good it would be. But, when we returned from our honeymoon, and began to live God's principles for marriage, we surged past our dreams into HIGH SIDE MARRIAGE.

As our book progresses into Mentoring, Problem Solving, etc., we again use High Side when we surge above our stretch expectations. The high side is getting closer to the principle as God designed it. It is a discovery beyond our wildest dream. The dream we shared for three years, which included waiting for intercourse, was now reality and direction setting. Jesus taught in Matthew 7:24 that we should "build our house upon a rock (God)" and He had gifted us with the shared faith to do just that. We had already experienced it on our honeymoon. Then (Matthew 7:25 continues) "the rain came down, the streams rose, and the winds blew and beat against that house, yet it did not fall." Our story was a bit different: sunburn, overheated car, mosquitos, and an engine problem. But neither of us even blinked, let alone feared or became stressed. Our house (marriage) was built on the rock (God) and secured forever. We left, cleaved, became one flesh and locked hands with God as our guide into Unity 101.

Principle 2 – One Flesh

I'll start this second principle with money, as it often impairs marriages. Immediately after we married, Sally and I pooled our money, knowing that from now on, everything is OURS, not yours and not mine. We were "one flesh" in everything, just as the Bible declares marriage to be. Therefore, we must adhere to that in the assets we have and the purposes they serve. Her assets were greater than my debt so we immediately used the modest excess to make a down payment on a house - OUR house. By summer's end, we said goodbye to the cats and moved into OUR HOME. It was not a mere structure called a house, but the love center in which our family would soon live. We had our old unreliable Buick and $105 cash. So we asked our cousins to give or lend us any unwanted furniture they had. It was grossly mismatched in appearance, but we saw it as beautiful. We were missing a few essentials, so we collected broken ones (stove, washer and dryer) and fixed them ourselves using our $105 to buy their parts. One flesh is a pervasive wonderful bond.

Principle 3 - Lead with Love

We now had to decide about grad school. Should we turn down the $500 to $520 per month job offers that would have let us replace the unreliable Buick? Sally joined into the decision with love and wisdom as God revealed its merit; God had imbedded principles into the universe He created, and I could learn about them at Case grad school. Our foundation would be stronger if our life story benefitted by knowing God's principles. Never in this five-year extension of college did Sally or I second guess that decision. The love God imparted into us was so strong that we can only recall one fight in 63 years, and we resolved that one with tears the same day it happened.

As we look back upon this five-year period, we can see the hand of God building the foundation upon which we would stand as He sent us forth into roles we could not even imagine.

After marriage, the next major objective we had looked forward to was FAMILY. Our first two children, Ken and Steve, were born while I was in grad school. Then the next three - Lynne, June and Jim – were born: five children in nine years. Sally's parents missed out on both of their expectations. They thought we'd have two children, and we had five. They thought we'd be paupers, and we were not; we had even replaced our old Buick with a car big enough for a family of seven, although we only had one car.

When Sally was pregnant with our first child, God sent a prophetic messenger to us. Bruce and Marilyn Clark, our close church friends, invited us to their home for dinner. Thereafter, Bruce took me out into their beautiful garden and challenged me, "Have you yet considered that God has arranged for you and Sally to be the most important two people in the shaping of this new life that He is now entrusting to you?!"

Expecting our first child, Ken

His message went deep into our hearts, like marriage before it. Thus, our second aspiration during our engagement had a Family High Side that we must seek out and do, just as we did with marriage when we were living in the maid's room. We immediately looked at our activities. We stopped playing golf (little kids don't play it) and replaced it with ice skating (families can do it together). Sally took this seriously, putting Ken in ice skates at two years old. Her logic was "if they can walk, they can skate." We made numerous small decisions like that. But, as with marriage, the really big decisions were those God guided us to embrace such as the next three principles:

Principle 4 – Love God

"Love the Lord your God with all your heart and with all your soul and with all your strength and with all your mind and love your neighbor as yourself," Luke 10:27. We must live our lives in such a way that our children see us as adherents to this principle. We won't do it perfectly, but we must do it intentionally. We must be the human manifestation of this love in both good and bad times. So, we will also need to involve them in a community that shares our commitment to God.

That, of course, is the church, and our Grace Baptist Church in Cleveland was a good one. We made it central to our out-of-the-house experiences for our children (Sunday AM and PM and Wednesday PM). We nearly always went to church. Even on trips, we sought out a local church. We also aligned ourselves with the church; not expecting it to be perfect but demonstrating our strong attachment to it as the "best" culture in town in which to raise children. In our home, we had daily devotions. You should not be surprised that our next principle is family.

Principle 5 – Love Family

You may recall that the first principle I referenced when we were seeking the high side for our marriage was Leave and Cleave, describing that as being vastly superior to just living in the same house. There are ways that other relationships among people can be uncommonly kind and supportive. That is precisely what happened during the Great Depression when I wrote "my mother and aunt bonded us cousins, not as a genetic word, but as a love-linked lifestyle to navigate depression / death / stroke. That love-linked lifestyle is a pervasive person-to-person environment in which selfishness is driven to near zero in a person." All five of our children are different from each other, yet all five arrived in this world with selfishness. The role that we had as parents was to be both a model for them and mentors coaching them into the ways that increase their love and caring for each other, while reducing the selfishness in them. They are, as I write, close friends of each other.

We knew that our children would devote huge portions of their lives to working, so we mentored them to be good workers. Once again, we sought to raise them to the high side. We emphasized first to be a Godly ethical person in every relationship; to your customers, your boss, your fellow workers, even your suppliers. We told them to let your word be true and your work be worthy. Sally began this before they could walk - if you take out a toy, put it back. Meanwhile, I stocked our house with tools so they all would fix it if they broke it and build it if they want it. Sally and I in both situations would help them and mentor them.

Sally and I took the Bruce Clark advice very seriously, deciding during her first pregnancy the whys and the hows and then improving them when Ken was born and parenting was for real. Some of the practical decisions that we made that added to God's principles were:

- Sally and I would agree to use the same methods, freedoms and boundaries.
- If a change was needed, we would work together to decide it, then both of us would conform to the change.
- Our children could get an immediate answer from either of us, and the parent who was not present would agree.
- When the parent who was not present had a different idea, we would candidly discuss it with just the two of us and (if warranted) make the decision differently the next time that issue came up.
- If a child asked a parent and got an answer, the child could appeal the decision, be listened to and (if warranted) that parent would change the decision.

- However, if the child is told "no" and then goes to the other parent, asks, and gets the answer the child preferred then, he or she would be punished. Playing a parent against a parent was not tolerated.

- Rational discussion with the child and either or both parents was encouraged (wisdom and love were gained).

- Children were encouraged to reach out, dream and discover. Childhood is the most fertile time of one's life to test, explore, innovate, etc.

- As such, the parent role is to stimulate, guide and mentor.

- We aimed to not crush their discovery process. When children reach kindergarten and are told to sit in a chair, don't chew gum, don't talk and to memorize the alphabet, their discovery and innovation diminishes.

- All children's questions are worthy of answers.

Principle 6 – Love Neighbor

Both Sally and I grew up with strong neighbor connections. I have already introduced you to my neighbor Kent Dean. We became neighbors during the Great Depression, played together, built crude wooden cars we could ride in, went through school together and hunted rabbits at his father's farm. Kent and I were the shortest two boys in our high school graduation class but fortunately, both of us added height during college. When Sally decided she should stop dating me during her senior year of high school, Kent became the boy she was dating when she finally fell in love with me. We are lifelong friends.

Sally likewise has a very close friend from early childhood, Joan Ellis. They met in grade school and took dance lessons in sixth grade together, with boys in suits and girls in dresses, both with white gloves on. This was to introduce them to what they'd need to attend Junior High school sock hops and after-school dances later. Joan and Sally were both in National Honor Society through school, but Joan was more into getting good grades and Sally was enjoying all sports available, often the captain of the teams. When they went to Miami University, they were roommates who lived and diligently studied together. Both girls were married in 1957, but Joan and Lowell Anderson still had one more year at Miami U. in married housing. Keith and Sally moved to grad school (Keith), and Sally became a secretary for the manager for the Glass Products Division of Diamond Alkali in Cleveland. They've never again lived in the same city as us, but stay connected via letters and phone.

The principle that God embodies in "Love your neighbor as yourself" is yet another high side principle that of course is much more inclusive than likeable friends like Kent and Joan. But it extends to whomsoever we interface with; challenging us to be caring and helpful, even to the state of love. It is not marital love but is a sincere caring for that person's needs. I've written about my mother's compassionate heart for people. Sally saw that in her and then chose to emulate her. She was already kind, but God was now promoting her to the high side and it became part of her lifelong career.

We thereby did befriend our neighbors. It was a decision, a behavior and a blessing as God broadened our friendships and coached us to meet the needs of the needy. During this era of Foundation, we did not use babysitters or pay childcare. Instead, we had a "point/per kid/per hour" set up for the mothers in our neighborhood to arrange for kids to play together. Sally could drop off our one, two, three or four kids at the Mary Bliss home or with any of the other eight or so mothers participating in this neighborhood exchange. Once a month, the mothers would get together, share their experiences, and see any imbalances of excessive drop-offs or excessive take-ins that should be corrected during the upcoming month. It was a great way to know our neighbors and to provide mutual care. But God's intent extended further than that. We needed also be a kind neighbor to the widow who lived next door who had needs and couldn't give back like moms were doing with the point system for kids. Indeed, the Bible explicitly and frequently commissions us "to meet the needs of the widows and the fatherless." As I was writing this, Sally has been delivering notes in the mailboxes of all the elderly and widows in our neighborhood, offering them help during the coronavirus pandemic we are experiencing in 2020.

Love is a verb: it is something we do. The highest attainment beyond God's love is the love we exchange with our spouse. But there is a love that is not sexual at all that we are to give to and to receive from our neighbors without any requirement for reciprocity. We bought a lake. We thought that we owned it but God took ownership of it by making it a kind and loving retreat for people to experience the beauty of His creation. We are its caretakers.

7

Principles, Mentoring and Problem Solving

Principles – A Definition

The high expectations and dreams that we had for both Marriage and Family were now coming to fruition. The first ways that we were attaining them were by living out the principles that we had pledged during our wedding. That link was obvious to both of us, so much so that the actual decision we made within that third principle was to learn more principles. But it was a high cost: Five more years of college so that I could learn the PRINCIPLES of metals, something so alien to your life story that you'd likely resist spending five minutes on it, let alone five years. But Sally and I had freshly learned the power of these six principles we described in the last chapter. As a young couple, we chose to invest in principles instead of a reliable car.

At this point, I want to define for you what I mean by principle.

A) <u>God's Principles for the Universe</u>. God designed many things to always happen exactly the same way, and they are inviolate (there is nothing anyone can do to change them). Example: gravity, and many aspects of physics, chemistry, and biology.

B) <u>God's Principles for us: Life Principles</u>. God designed them and revealed them in the Bible. They are the best way to live but are violated by people extensively.

C) <u>Principles designed by people</u>. They are legion in number, often useful and sometimes harmful. Frequently violated.

As a Christian, I believe that God gave us A & B to enable our life story and yours to experience the high side of marriage, family, and career within our life. That's why Sally and I mutually agreed to those five years to deepen our understanding of principles. Thereby, our foundation became: stand firmly upon A and B, then use C for areas God didn't describe. My PhD education taught me the science that undergirded my engineering bachelor's degree. I define science as "the extent thus far that men and women have discovered the principles God used when He created the universe and those who live within it."

As a Christian, I believe that God gave us A & B to enable our life story and yours to experience the high side of marriage, family, and career within our life.

For those three years between falling in love and marrying, we managed our impatience with the two dreams of Marriage and Family. Then the very foundation of our lives was firmed up; God guided us to His design for both, just by finding and conforming to the six of His principles I just described in the previous chapter. We now experienced them for real and they carry us beyond our most extravagant dreams. Then, as He stretched us to "Love Neighbors," He gifted us with incredible friendships; on our block, in our church, at Case, etc. They were and are legion. What a bonus.

Could it now be that God would carry this over into Careers? Of course, it was the rest of His plan He had for us.

But I will defer describing principles impacting my career until later when I cover them during the 10 positions of my Alcoa career. For now, let's look again at our wedding, this time naming every time that a God-Life Principle was being used to frame our marriage: 29 are listed, some of them more than once. All of them are "as spoken" by Bob Rogers or "as sung" by Lynn Rogers. Principles of God are usually clear and always profound. They lead us to HIGH SIDE life stories.

***

Marriage as an Example of Principles

As you read these, I challenge you to be alert to these two features: First, that each is a stand-alone single LIFE PRINCIPLE worthy of our use and your use in the ways Sally and I used them in the preceding chapter. Then Second: their relevance is beyond one-by-one use in that the 29 are a set, a system and a lovingly integrated master plan that God linked together when He designed marriage and imparted to us such that we could experience love. The attributes of this love are: like the Christ / church union, happy home, joy, peace, tender, sacred, comfort, honor, only unto her, for life, true, lawful, cleave, respect and obey, faithfulness, eternity, enduring, imperishable, same path, same lodging, same God, traveling God's Kingdom on Earth, as witnesses of God, peace of heart, Jesus within us, happiness, seeking God's will. God connected all of these together like the instruments of an orchestra that together make harmonious music, in this case, LOVE.

The actual words spoken in our wedding were 29 Principles sequenced as follows:

1. God attended our wedding – overseeing everything.
2. We were joined in holy matrimony – instituted by God.
3. Matrimony is an honorable estate – God designed it that way.
4. The Keith/Sally union is mystical – like the Christ/Church union is.

5. We're to enter the union reverently and discreetly – in the fear of God.

2-5. It is into this holy estate – that Keith and Sally come now to be drawn.

6. Love and love alone – will avail as the foundation of a happy home.

7. If Sally and Keith keep the vows and obey God – our life will be full of joy and the home we established will abide in peace.

8. No other ties are more tender or sacred – than these marriage vows.

9. Keith; will you take Sally – to be your wedded wife.

10. Will you love, comfort, honor and keep Sally – in sickness and health.

11. Will you forsake all others – keep thee only unto her for life

9-11. "Yes" to those "Will you's."

9-11. Sally said "Yes" too.

12. Sally's father and mother gave me Sally – to leave and cleave.

13. Keith; will you take Sally – as your true and lawful wife.

14. Will you love, cherish, honor and protect her, cleaving unto her – until God by death separates you.

13-14. Keith responded "I do."

13-14. Sally said yes too, but "respect" was changed to "obey."

13-14. Then we repeated the above words from memory – forgetting some.

15. In both memorized vows, we added – I pledge thee my troth.

15a. Troth is a pledge based on truth and faithfulness.

16. We both exchanged rings – as tokens of love for each other.

17. The ring is a circle – the emblem of eternity.

18. The gold is least tarnished – most enduring.

19. The ring shows faith – lasting and imperishable.

20. The pledge shows union – only separated by death.

21. We pledged to travel life together – same path, same lodging.

22. We pledged to share relationships – thy people shall be my people, thy God my God.

21-22. Then, based upon these pledges, we were pronounced husband and wife.

21-22. In the name of the Father, Son and Holy Spirit.

AMEN

23. Then Pastor Lynn sang part of the Lord's Prayer (Kingdom come on earth).

Then Pastor Bob Rogers prayed:

Thank you God – for today's blessing and benediction.

24. Use the lives of Keith and Sally to be a witness of thyself.

25. With peace of heart, rest upon the assurance that Jesus is their guide.

24-25. Then remember the day and hour – with real happiness.

26. Living their lives – searching out your will for them.

27. May they ever rejoice – because this assembly honored the marriage.

25-27. For it is in Jesus' precious name – we pray with thanksgiving.

AMEN.

28. Keith, so love Sally in such a way – that it will be easy for her

29. To reverence and obey you.

I now take pleasure to present to you, Mr. and Mrs. Keith Turnbull.

Our wedding was not routine nor was it a show of color and beauty. It was God doing His workmanship upon us so that our life story would be a love story, using His Life Principles via God/Family/Career. PRAISE GOD.

With Principles as our guideposts for life - the very definition for High Side - there are two "how to" processes that I have chosen to pair with them: Mentoring and Problem Solving.

It was God doing His workmanship upon us so that our life story would be a love story...

The role of Case? A massive breakthrough. The pathway to Alcoa? Amazing. The role of mentoring? Brace yourself, our life story is poised to attain another high side.

***

Mentoring – The High Side

Mentoring is a commonly used word, such that you likely have a meaning already in mind. Perhaps it is a verb describing a process (mentoring), by which a person transfers knowledge to someone else. Or perhaps it is a noun (mentor), the person who is providing the knowledge. Or perhaps it is a training manual, written by a mentoring expert such that the reader can read and thereby know. And then, of course, one can just "Google it" and get a great answer with visuals such that the answer is carried out before your very eyes.

All of those are true, but there is more; something that reckons all the way back to Bruce Clark's God-given advice when he explained fatherhood to me; "God has arranged for us (Keith & Sally) to be the most important two people in the shaping of this new life that He (God) was now entrusting to us." What an incredible insight! Mentoring in its richest form is a people process with a caring dimension, not merely a transactional event like how to cook a recipe. I wrote earlier that Bruce Clark's message went deep into Sally's and my hearts. Sometimes mentoring is between husband and wife. Pastor Bob Rogers' last comment prior to his "meet Mr. & Mrs. Keith Turnbull" was "Remember, Keith, to love Sally in such a way that it will be easy for her to reverence and obey you." During my Alcoa career, every one of my bosses cared about me and built me up as a person as part of their mentoring behavior. That is why I chose to define mentoring to the depth I have experienced it so that you will understand my meteoric movement from scientist to executive vice president.

Mentoring in its richest form is a people process with a caring dimension...

I confess to you that this is the fifth time I've written and rewritten this definitional dimension of mentoring. The high side of mentoring is attained when knowledge, wisdom, methods, practices, etc., are transferred between a mentor and mentee who care about each other. That sentence is simple yet profound. So, why then did I have to write it five times? Because there is yet one more dimension to high side mentoring that is rarely known or described. It is:

Mentoring into Autonomous

Autonomous is a big word that you experience, but don't pay much attention to. It means something is happening without you having to think about it. You use it when you're driving and turn on cruise control. Thereafter, you can remove your foot from the accelerator and the car will continue at your present speed regardless of the hills and valleys you are driving through. Pilots fly airplanes on autopilot and can even land a plane using autopilot. Autonomous simply means that we have some operation that happens without us having to handle it, mentally nor physically. Within your body, at the very moment of conception in your mother's womb, God turned on a whole set of autonomous processes that are extremely important to you BUT that you do not have to manage. Examples include your heart, your liver, your kidneys, etc. Then, amazingly, God put in an internal army of white blood cells that rush to your defense every time that you are sick or wounded. Then, God built into our bodies a whole set of repair processes so that everything I've just mentioned has been repairing itself within my body for 85 years so far.

Furthermore, as an amazing gift from God, He has given us the privilege to add other autonomous functions to our body. For example, you mentored into your fingers the motions they will perform when you send a text message. See for yourself. Rotate your smart phone 180 degrees and try to type a message. It's hard. Why? Because your fingers were mentored to carry out a particular motion for the letter "c" and a different motion for "a" and still another motion for "t" every time your brain thinks "cat." You subconsciously mentored that into your fingers by repetitive actions. Singers do that with their mouth, lips and tongues, violinists with their fingers, and hockey players with their hockey sticks.

Let's call this important aspect of mentoring "learn by doing." A hockey enthusiast can hear lectures, read manuals and consult Google forever and never attain the requisite competence to control a puck with a hockey stick, let alone score a goal. High side mentoring recognizes this and sees to it that the functions of the mentee that must move into autonomous capability (like your fingers sending text messages) are attained properly. To get to the high side, it is done respectfully. Finally, since we as people have the capacity to be evil, we must avoid nurturing wrong processes into an autonomous state. In the musical South Pacific, Lieutenant Cable fell in love with a Polynesian woman from the Bali Hai Island and then cried out passionately against the autonomous dimension of racial prejudice:

> *You've got to be taught to hate and fear.*
> *You've got to be taught from year to year,*
> *It's got to be drummed in your dear little ear.*
> *You've got to be carefully taught.*
> *You've got to be taught to be afraid*
> *Of people whose eyes are oddly made,*
> *and people whose skin is a different shade.*
> *You've got to be carefully taught.*
> *You've got to be taught before it's too late,*
> *Before you are six or seven or eight,*
> *To hate all the people your relatives hate,*
> *You've got to be carefully taught!*

I trust now that this description of mentoring makes sense to you. I confess that I learned it gradually during my 40-year Alcoa career and thereafter imperfectly gifted it to my mentees and, of course, to our children. But perhaps my definition has a learning lesson that you can use in your life story far earlier than I did.

***

Problem Solving – High Side

I trust that you found value in this pause in our life story writing to teach and to emphasize the important Learning Lessons of Principles and Mentoring. I took them to their high sides because they can have such a large impact upon your life story and the people whom you are impacting. The third is Problem Solving and this one links up with Principles and Mentoring in awesome ways.

The implication of linking the three is so great that I've chosen to tell you the answer first and cover the details secondly. I suspect that you, like me, know that problems are bad. They mess things up, cost money, delay us and often are hard to solve. True indeed! But, it is less so when you use the principles of the universe and the life principles to diagnose the cause and to simplify the solution. Also, it is less so if mentoring as I have described it is the intent and reality among the people who are solving the problem. Also, it is less so if the method of problem solving is of the type I will next describe.

In fact, when you put these three together, the sting of the problem can become less than the positive excitement of solving it quickly into a solution closer to the perfection of the principles, while teaming with people who build each other up. Problems solved this way can even be POSITIVE.

The importance of Problem Solving linked to Principles and Mentoring is so very high that I've chosen to describe it in stages beginning with childhood and progressing to the adult high side version of Problem Solving.

***

Children Solve Problems

Let's begin by considering how children do problem solving. Infants burst onto the scene using crying, facial expressions, kicking legs and flailing arms to recruit mother, father, sibling or whoever will come when the problem is hunger, loaded diaper, tiredness, or just plain anger. The problem-solving methods actually work quite well. Soon, they progress to perpetual discovery using seeing, touching, hearing, tasting, and smelling – all five senses – to assess, eat, destroy or hug whatever it is they are discovering. When a discovery sprays them, scratches them or knocks them over, they advance to their built-in problem solving to fight or flight. In simple terms, since they dislike sprays, scratches or knock overs, they either retreat or push back against; the sibling who sprayed them, the cat who scratches them or the large dog that knocked them over.

Now, if you watch them carefully, you will see them discerning that sibling CAUSES, cat CAUSES and large dog CAUSES are different and therefore require three different solutions. The sibling cause was teasing, the cat cause was the child squeezing the cat, whereas the dog cause was simply incidental. God implants these problem-solving ways in each child. Parents respond very differently to the problems of children thereby strongly influencing which problem-solving method the child will further develop. Sadly, as children grow up within our culture, we frequently repress their childhood intense exploration that was leading to rapid discovery. They are taught that making mistakes is bad, even embarrassing. So they have to cut back on their discovery process that was usually revealing something that was good. Why? Because they would be punished if the discovery revealed something bad.

I have written those observable behaviors about children because Sally, you and I solve our adult problems in ways that were strongly influenced by our parents, friends, teachers, enemies and environments.

Not so for the turtles in our lake; their mother buries her eggs and leaves them. Then they hatch, walk to the nearest water and fend for themselves. They have protective maneuvers like jumping off a log if a person comes near, which are completely innate. Life is more severe for our largemouth bass; the mother lays the eggs and guards them until they hatch. When they grow into reasonable-size minnows, she eats them. Ducklings fare far better; the mother lays the eggs, sits on them for about 30 days to keep them warm and then protects the ducklings until they are fully grown. However, the duck mating process is 100% promiscuous such that neither the male nor female knows which male fathered which egg so the fathers play no role in raising the ducklings. Canadian geese are the best of our water creature examples. They pair up for life, are certain about who the parent is, are protective of each other and raise their goslings in a two-goose collaborative way.

I've listed these four to show you the extremes of nature between animals and offspring so that you're receptive to the reality that we as parents strongly impact our children and their problem solving. Recall that my father was stubborn and from that, I did the opposite. Yet he very effectively taught me how to solve the problem of an uninhabitable house. Thereafter, when we bought our house, I learned to solve all of the upgrade problems such as toilets, showers and sinks. He also taught me to solve problems of farming and fixing broken things. Meanwhile, my mother was mentoring me to solve people problems; relationship problems, confession / repent / reconcile problems, love problems, and even dating problems.

God designed humans not as turtles, bass or ducks, but somewhat with the goose template. Then He added huge measures of love, brain power, physical strength, etc. such that we could massively outperform the goose. Then He gave us the Bible as a written instruction on how to live, if we choose to, and an offer to be our constant live-in counselor, if we let Him. Then He granted us freedom of choice, which we often use to impair our relationship with our spouse or to compromise our roles as parents. That is why the frequent checking to see what God Principles apply to each situation helps us with children and at home and work. Since God's Principles are the science type and the life principle type, we can get both right answers and right relationships.

You, Sally and I are vastly different than the inhabitants of our lake. We would die at birth if no one cared for us. So also at age 1, 2 or 3. God designed us to be interdependent for a decade or more such that you, Sally and I each have a way that we customarily solve problems. After this many years, some aspects are autonomous, repeated so many times that it is our instantaneous first reaction to a problem. Then, beyond autonomous, we have the many other elements that we think through to discern and to solve. The autonomous skips the brain. The others use the brain. So I ask you, How DO you solve problems? How did your parents solve problems? How are you teaching your children to solve problems? How does your school solve problems, or your workplace?

These are questions well worth answering. What would you do with the child who was crying, kicking legs and flailing arms if you were at home? Would it be different if it happened at the grocery store? It was for Sally. At home, she would have the time and environment to find out the problem and its cause. But at the store, she would try to calm her child and to exit the store. Why? Because she was embarrassed that she couldn't keep her child from crying in public and she had learned ways to quiet the child temporarily and defer problem solving until she got to her car. Yet, we have huge problems in our schools today because children generate chaos such that teachers can't teach and children don't learn and thereby seriously impair their futures.

With all of these insights into problem solving (or not solving), what does my life story reveal about problem solving? Quite a bit, because I am intentionally seeking God's Principles and Mentoring methods to diagnosis and to solve problems. That's why I've paused in our life story to share with you the problem solving method that I grew into by the time that I began my career in Alcoa and then added to during those 40 years.

Engineering is a disciplined profession in the same way as the health care domain of doctors and nurses. Each has a problem-solving method they most commonly use as follows:

Health Care Method	Engineer Method
Observe	Problem
Ask Questions	Cause
Form a Hypothesis	Solution
Make a Prediction	Action
Test the Hypothesis	Measure
Iterate (Repeat)	

I am not an expert in the doctor/nurse methods, but I asked several healthcare providers and each gave me essentially the same answer of the method on the left column of the table. Their hypothesis is the central intent for solving a patient's health problem or developing a vaccination for the COVID-19 virus. It is the formulation of a possible SOLUTION to the problem that they are addressing. They formulate the solution by OBSERVING (your general health or COVID-19 indicators) and by ASKING very targeted QUESTIONS relevant to problems such as these so that they can distinguish which one it likely is. Then they generate their HYPOTHESIS (the "indicated" solution) and the PREDICTED consequences (extent of healing and possible side effects) that they then administer to the patient and TEST the consequences. If necessary, they REPEAT. Based upon this test result, the second hypothesis may be needed, and perhaps a third hypothesis, even fourth, as they fight a particularly difficult cancer or virus. Their domain is primarily biology, with some chemistry.

As an engineer and scientist, my domain has some biology, but is generally more connected to physics and chemistry. As such, I have the intent to solve problems with the five-step method on the right side of the table above that has definitions as follows:

1. Problem – what is the pain?
2. Cause – what is the genesis of the pain?
3. Solution – how might we stop this pain?
4. Actions – what things must we do based upon this solution?
5. Measure – the pain is thereby gone.

The set of five is called a hypothesis. Let's look at a simple example using the problem of a car that won't start.

1. Problem – Car won't start.
2. Cause – Dead battery because lights were left on.

3. Solution – Recharge the battery.

4. Actions – Turn off the lights, safely attach charger to the correct battery terminals, charge the battery.

5. Measures – Charger signals that the battery is fully charged. Car starts.

Hopefully, those two descriptions adequately describe the five-step process that many of us have grown up with. The risk we all face is that we will forget that all five are needed or decide that we've become wise enough that we can skip steps, sometimes three of them. An example of skipping three would be: the problem is inventory and the objective is to reduce it by 30% - just do it.

As I disciplined myself to use all five steps, problem solving became easier, faster and more effective. Then, when I sought out the Principles related to the Problem, I could better understand the problem, cut quickly through the mere symptoms, spot the root cause as it relates to the principles and then discern a superior solution nestled within its principles. Please take seriously the importance of these uncommonly used words.

So where do I find the PRINCIPLES? That's easy – they're the Universal Principles that God put in place for Him to govern the universe like physics, chemistry, and biology. Of course, they are also the Life Principles that God gave us for our high side behaviors as humans; honesty, kindness, ethics, morals, love, grace, respect. Please do not be scared by the physics that is involved in the car lightbulb and the chemistry that is involved in the battery. It was sufficient this time to know the lightbulb as on/off and the battery as charged/discharged. I mentioned them to encourage you that simply using a principle adds value.

For the car, the Principle was "electrical." Good, knowing that fact casts aside the chaos of the many other possible reasons the car will not start. Within the electrical system are bulb principles, switch principles, wire principles and battery principles. Not bad, only four to go. The battery was dead. A light switch was left in the "on" position. The collateral causes were the dead battery, which was drained because the lights were left on. The root cause was that the switch was left on.

Simultaneous to the switch and battery principles are God's other set of principles, the Life Principles, pertaining to all of the people involved. I start problem solving with "What," not "Who," because "Who" is often threatening. Let's imagine people in our car scenario. Sue, who couldn't start the car, is afraid she caused the issue and that she will be late for work. John notices her fears and immediately offers to drive her to work. He relieves both of her fears as he drives, and thanks her for finding the problem. David, who knows very little about electricity, offers that there was no sound when Sue tried to start the car. For Sam, that observation markedly narrowed the possible cause list, so he immediately tested the battery. It was dead, so he attached a charger to the battery. The headlights lit up. John looked and saw the switch in the "on" position. They had traced the problem to the Root Cause. The headlights had been left on overnight. Everyone celebrated.

Sue, John, David and Sam were friends. All four were unafraid to speak up. None were accusative. Their friendship grew deeper. Problem solving can be that way. That's why I solve them using God's Universal and Life Principles linked together when I engage in problem solving. It is a huge part of effective mentoring.

8

Career Intervention

As I approached PhD. graduation in 1962, I was fully aware that I had prepared myself into a very narrow field: a research scientist in a metals research lab. But I was perfectly comfortable with that because I had experienced it during my summer internships in the Alcoa Research Lab and in my daytime work at Case for five years when I was doing research and teaching laboratories. I was 26 years old and had nine years of college education.

But, from God's perspective, my resume would read quite differently than the one above. My salvation was at age seven and five years later I successfully cast aside the baggage that had been wrongly attached to it. I learned God's version of collaboration as we cousins navigated depression/death/stroke as a love-linked lifestyle. I had chosen the wife God intended for me and then learned patience and persistence during seven years of dating. We dated before Sally's salvation so God put an evangelist in her religion class to close that gap. Then right after our wedding, we quickly used His principles to upscale both our marriage and family to levels far above the dreams we had during our engagement. Oh yes, He had so intrigued us about God's principles that we spent five years learning the ones He used for metals and related technologies like stress/strain that are required for airplanes to fly. While I was learning metal principles, Sally had a two-year taste of business, and then God launched her lifetime career of loving and nurturing children. My mother was Sally's mentor for motherly love for our first two children, but my mother died shortly after my graduation in 1963.

As you will see as we describe the rest of our life story, every word in those two resumes was relevant to the careers that follow.

I interviewed with some companies prior to my Ph.D. graduation, but I was primarily interested in NASA (the National Aeronautics and Space Administration). As the Cold War progressed, Russia surged past the USA in their missile development by launching Sputnik, the first satellite to go into orbit around the earth, weighing 64 pounds. The United States had no such capability and was struggling to design one that would only be 16 pounds. National concerns were so high that the government was striving to increase the population of

Ph.D.'s in engineering or science. They contacted my brother who was a professor introducing a technology curriculum into the Baptist's newly formed Cedarville College. He had a BS and MS in chemistry, a Master of Divinity and was taking night classes for a master's in physics. All of these made sense for the important role he had there. The government offered to pay his current salary plus all of his college expenses if he would switch to full time on the fastest path to a PhD. He accepted the offer, discontinued his physics work at Ohio State and moved from Cedarville to Cleveland so he could get a PhD in chemistry, his fastest path because he already had an MS in chemistry.

My purpose for writing that part of Bruce's life story was so that you would understand why I was choosing to go into the NASA lab, a mere seven miles from our house. Professor

Jack Wallace

Jack Wallace was my boss and mentor for my five years of graduate school. I was a research assistant, working 40 hours per week on projects paid for by the industry that served the double purpose of meeting the sponsor's need and generating my MS thesis and PhD thesis that Case required. All of my classes were in the evening. Professor Wallace was a "full service" mentor developing me as a scientist, experimentalist, pragmatist, doer, writer, speaker and hockey adviser. He even told me "It's time for you to grow up and stop getting these

109

hockey injuries," advice that I ignored until age 81. When I neared graduation for my PhD, he called me in for some explicit mentoring:

> Professor Wallace: What is this I hear about you wanting to go to work at NASA?
>
> Keith: Yes, it is very exciting. The space projects they're doing will humans into orbit and I can be part of that.
>
> Wallace: So, what about Alcoa?
>
> Keith: Well... this NASA opportunity looks really good.
>
> Wallace: That may be so, but you didn't even interview with Alcoa. Is that true?
>
> Keith: Yes, but.......
>
> Wallace: Sorry, but you cannot choose to NOT interview with Alcoa. The relationship between Case and Alcoa is too important for you to impair it.
>
> Keith: *Not speaking but thinking "I haven't yet passed my verbal thesis exam and I can't graduate without passing that. Professor Wallace chairs that committee!"*
>
> Wallace: You MUST interview Alcoa. You do not have to accept their job offer, but you must interview them!

After that meeting, Professor Wallace resumed the discussion he was having with Vice President Kent Van Horn, about which I knew nothing. I had been tagged as a "must hire" by Alcoa after my two summer internships. Van Horn was a diligent overseer of hiring research scientists into his lab.

Professor Wallace shared with Van Horn about my family, my Cleveland roots, etc. Alcoa gave me two job offers; one at the huge research lab in Pittsburgh and the other to the Cleveland research lab reporting to Bob Lemon, an outstanding boss I knew from interning, with job content they knew I would like and (of course) the merit of staying with family in Cleveland.

Then Professor Wallace gave me his final counsel:

Wallace: Has it occurred to you yet that you will always have a boss?

Keith: *I was surprised by the question, but the answer was* "No."

Wallace: Well, you will. And there are good bosses and bad bosses and you won't do well under a bad boss. You'll quit and go elsewhere.

Keith: *Puzzled.*

Wallace: You know that I've worked in industry and for the government.

Keith: Right.

Wallace: Well, when industry has a bad boss, they see it and either move the person out of a manager role or fire them. But in government, they just leave them where they are. I hated being trapped beneath a bad boss when I worked in the government and so will you.

Both Alcoa job offers were really attractive. I accepted the Cleveland offer and never looked back. Nine years later, I transferred to the much larger research lab in Pittsburgh. I had chosen a company with high ethics and very intentional mentoring.

The United States caught up to Russia, orbited the earth, and then landed astronauts on a round trip to the moon. So who is Van Horn and what does he have to do with Case and my life story? I will share with you later the information of the Case/Alcoa connection and Dr. Van Horn's role. But first, let us overview my 40-year career. I had 10 Alcoa positions in 40 years and will describe all 10 in sequential steps. Then later, I will pair each interval with its God/Family counterparts. But I first must have one extra write-up for Family/God because those two were active during the five-year Foundation era when I had not yet been hired by Alcoa.

It all fits together.

9

Family – Birthing and Learning 1959 to 1962

This God/Family segment of our next 40 years begins with the birth of our first child, Ken, in November 1959. You must recall that on April 3, 1954, Sally and I were so separated that marriage and family were zero. Then, on April 4, Sally fell in love with me and everything changed and by the end of that month, we were fixated on a two-theme dream: marriage and family. God now granted us our wish. As you read earlier, He used Bruce and Marilyn Clark to focus our attention on parenting our child.

When Sally reached her third month of pregnancy, she was fired by Diamond Alkali because it was "company policy" for mothers-to-be. So be it; God had a much more important career for her as mother (times five), loving mentor to thousands of children and chief family builder. I worked five days per week and by Ken's seventh birthday, about three of those days each week were out of town on business.

Left to right: Keith, Steve, Lynne, June and Ken

She really took her role seriously, using her first seven years finding the right location and designing the right house so that it would be uncommonly child friendly; not elegant, not flashy, but absolutely child friendly. Then she engaged all four of our children (Jim was not born yet) in its construction as soon as Ken and Steve came home from school each day. She was mentoring them through "learn by doing" even with 1 ½-years-old June at the construction site.

I launched this segment of our book by going immediately into the family development portion because it is so very crucial and began halfway through our Foundation era,

2 ½ years prior to my career at Alcoa. Both of us really loved being parents, took the diaper process in stride and quickly reached Sally's goal to have two children, which occurred with Steve's birth two years after Ken. My parents had two children, Sally's parents had two children and Sally's mother had counseled Sally that two is the ideal number. But we really loved these first two and decided to continue; so one year later Lynne was born, then two years later June, and finally four years later Jim. When the third was born, we became a crowd and when the fifth was born, we became a mob, at least in the eyes of Sally's mother. She had fancy glassware at low levels on glass shelves in her dining room, poised for destruction if our mob invaded. Our visits to the Ewing house were almost always picnics outside with occasional trips into the house to the bathroom. My mother was the opposite; you already know that her house was anything but elegant. Her approach was "bring them in, any time, for any length, without any warning." She was the ultimate childcare choice. Sadly, she died shortly after Lynne was born. But remember, Sally saw my mother's love before our own children were born and had chosen to learn it and do it. Now she was learning firsthand how to carry that strength forward into her role as a new mother.

God gifted me with an incredible wife and He now grew her into a loving and competent mother so that she could fulfill His assignment for her in the lives of thousands of children beyond her own. Do you now see why she designed and built our house primarily for children? Then, a few years later, God gave her a second chance. He transferred us from Cleveland to Pittsburgh so she could design out whatever constraints that were within the first house and locate the new one on its own lake. Oh yes, and add a bedroom because Jim, our fifth child, was born after the first house. Sally's mother was right – we were a "mob" by the time we were a family of

seven so we needed to hang out with other mob families, those with three or more so we didn't scare people with the conventional one or two. But our house made it easy. Sally knew the needs of children and put them and me second, right behind her love for God.

As for me, I was the head of the marriage as God prescribed. But I also strove to make it easy for Sally to be my wife and mother of our children. I was mentoring my wife by lovingly assisting her to become all that God intended her to be. Per the God-given principle, I was doing this lovingly and sacrificially. I was not perfect but I was intentional. We were covenant bound to raise them together per the principle of one flesh by which everything became "ours." Of course, I gave Ken a hockey stick for his first birthday as a symbol of the community we would share. Our oldest granddaughter Jessica and her husband Ted are following our first birthday tradition with ice skating gifts, as are our other grandchildren. Why? Because families ice skate together, while golf is individual and low in mentoring.

As we now move into the 40 year/10 position Alcoa part of our life story, it is important to lead off with an updated summary of our position with God. God made us to be "of one faith," what an incredible gift! We immediately attended church together. Not just that we went to the same building, attended the same service and sat in the same pew. NO, much more! We had become "one flesh," that spiritual biblical term that we read and began to comprehend when we made a covenant before God to be husband and wife "till death do we part." But more so, we bonded heart to heart and had God as our constant companion. He had plans for us massively beyond anything we had ever dreamed. Watch them unfold during our 63 years of marriage thus far.

Our next five years were a period of intense growth in us individually and as a couple. Sally had gained salvation and a very clear recognition of who God is and what it means for her to now be a child of God. But her upbringing did not give her much knowledge of the Bible. Although she knew how to pray, she was frightened to pray out loud among adults. Yet God prepared her for a 50-year plus role teaching and mentoring thousands of fifth grade girls. Of course, God backfilled her Bible knowledge level from "light" to "cum laude" in Bible, far beyond her college cum laude in business.

Meanwhile, during these five years, God grew me from attender, to teacher, to leader within our Grace Baptist Church. Our church grew and God prepared me to become chairman of the building committee in the next season of our life story.

Neither of us have seminary training. I'm the only male cousin who didn't travel that route to become a pastor. But God bonded us as husband and wife as you have just read and dispatched us into lay leader roles that were awesome. Both of us serve from our hearts, Sally with our children, thousands of children and whoever she meets and greets. She is an ambassador of God. I serve in a lesser role than her as chairman of our church's Building Committee and Operations Board.

Can you believe it? The two of us who yearned for children and family when we fell in love on that day in 1954 now have a family tree of 55, all of whom we love deeply. We have never been perfect parents, but we tried hard, as we did as cousins in our childhood. We sought God's help. All of our children are Christians, beneficiaries of Sally's faith and love.

Both of us have had meteoric careers, speeding rapidly into uncharted space. Sally, who at first was afraid to pray in public, became inordinately strong, praying from her heart and seeing her children, all children, and thence all people as precious to God. She loves our 20 grandchildren and their 12 spouses, and they all know it. All 32 are Christians. Then there are the great grandchildren (11 and counting) upon whom Sally bestows her love. In college, Sally majored in business.

She went to work in business and was terminated 21 months later because of the company's policy for women once they reached their third month of pregnancy. God had a more important job for her in Family.

I believe that the best way for you to understand the rest of our life story is to separate the Career portion from the God/Family portion. Moving back and forth among the three as I have done so far would make them hard for you to understand the tightly connected steps of my Alcoa career.

The overview of my career unfolded in 10 stages, starting as a research scientist and attaining executive vice president of a $33 billion company. I look back in amazement at the scope that God was entrusting to me and the leadership acumen that each of the leaders of Alcoa had as they mentored me into each of the 10 positions. With all of this came wealth; money God entrusted to Sally and me, not to live lavishly, but to be stewarded as He would direct.

10

Alcoa – Perpetual Mentoring 1962 to 2003

I now take you on a fast trip through my 40-year Alcoa career by simply listing the 10 positions I had, the work I did and the people who mentored me.

The first two are the "learn by doing" recruitment assessment by Alcoa.

- Summer intern – on the job training to sort candidates in 1956 – Walter Sicha (Alcoa division chief)
- Recruitment – in the steps of the master in 1957 - Kent Van Horn – who discovered the science of metals

The next 10 are: Position - the Role - the Mentor(s)

1. Research engineer – bridge rail posts and more in 1962 - Bob Lemon, Al Montgomery, Kent Van Horn
2. Launcher – of a new titanium forging business in 1965 -

Al Favre, Bob Bergdaul, Jerry Hosner

3. Section Head – innovation SWAT team to recycle aluminum cans in 1971 - Bob Spear

4. Manager of research, ingot casting division - 44 of 44 in top half in 1974 - Bob Spear

5. A director of research lab – leading technologies of all types in 1979 - Jim Dowd

6. Manager, business planning – corporate wide in 1980 - Harry Goern

7. Director of technology planning – "That we not be steel" in 1982 - Marv Gantz – invent it, we can't tell you how

8. Vice president – technology planning – we invented it in 1986 - Jay Keyworth, Kim Clark, Kent Bowen, Robert Mehrabian, Ben Streetman and Bob Hornbeck of Alcoa

9. Executive vice president – strategy, quality and IT in 1991 - Paul O'Neill – brilliant, wise, ethical CEO

10. Executive vice president – the Toyota Production System in 1996 - Hajime Ohba (Toyota Master), John Marushin

Quite a trip that I was privileged to travel. Now that you know the scope, let's go back and repeat these 10 steps to tease out possible learning lessons for you.

My advice to you is that you primarily focus on the human aspects of my 10 career stories. See the aluminum, titanium, research and business aspects as the CONTEXT, not the MESSAGE. See God using the core of me that He molded as Great Depression COUSINS that He leveraged via mentors vastly beyond the mere metallurgy I studied for nine years. The "people" dimension is useful in all aspects of Sally's and my Life Story and in yours.

I began my 40-year career with Alcoa immediately after my Ph.D. graduation as a research engineer in the Alcoa Research Lab in Cleveland, Ohio. But, in a sense, my career began during the Roaring Twenties because that is when metallurgy ceased being an art. From the beginning of time, no one knew that there were underlying principles for metals. They therefore learned how to use metals by trial and error, and then passed their practices forward from a master to an apprentice.

Scientists then began using a new tool called X-ray diffraction that they aimed at a metal surface, expecting it to simply reflect as randomly ordered particles would. BUT IT DID NOT – it diffracted (rebounded off the metal in distinct bands like a rainbow does). Eureka! Metals are, and always were, crystalline with atoms lined up in distinct rows. God's design since time's beginning was now discovered. Where in the world did that happen - in Cleveland, at Case in the laboratory where I subsequently studied. Who discovered it - two men, the son and a mentoree who were living in the house of the department chairman Count Van Horn. Their names are Kent Van Horn (the son) and Zay Jeffries (the mentoree). What did they do with their findings - took them to the Cleveland Alcoa plant and launched the Alcoa Research Lab.

Kent Van Horn

Do you see now why I said my hiring was amazing? Kent Van Horn's father was a superb mentor that he passed on to his son, who continued that leadership method as he moved from Case to Alcoa and ramped up his lab to nearly 800 people. Look again at my 40-year career on a single page. I had 10 positions in those 40 years and was mentored in all except one, which couldn't be mentored because it had never been done before.

I remember all of these mentors. Look up and down the list at the breadth of the roles in which I worked. They are so different from my education that I could easily have failed, but in each one, Alcoa provided training and a domain-specific mentor. I will describe each of the positions to you and will share the learning lessons that are most likely to apply to your life story. Then I will share an overarching description showing how the individual roles converge into an overall system-wide advantage.

***

Step 1: Bridge Rail Posts

The first assignment I received was to solve the bridge post problem that caused the Federal Highway Administration to ban aluminum guard rail posts from all federal highways.

It was a real-life problem and it was mine to solve. Help

was available from the adjoining mechanical engineering department if I requested it. The posts were cast aluminum heat-treated to fairly high strength. They usually stopped a car, but sometimes broke, such that a car could fall off a bridge.

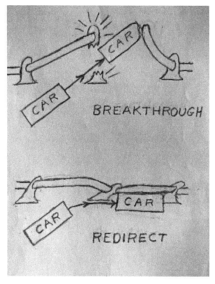

The science breakthroughs of Jeffries and Van Horn enabled me to change (at my will) the rupture performance of the post. So I invented a new alloy, A340, which relinquished strength to gain ductility so the post would bend instead of break. A340 was so bendable and rubberlike that it would bend under impact and would share the impact load with the rail and thence the two adjoining posts. This greatly reduced the impact force upon the post rail system because the car was redirected, instead of stopped, and passengers incurred less injury because their car ran alongside the railing, instead of stopping abruptly or breaking through and falling.

We rented the runway of an abandoned airport and crashed remote operated cars at various speeds and approach angles for the Federal Highway staff to observe. They reinstated aluminum posts with the specification that they had to be of the A340 alloy. My boss Bob Lemon watched and coached me, but never upstaged me. I was launched into my Alcoa career and anxious for my next assignment.

The learning lessons to share with you are numerous. My purpose for writing this first of 10 positions is for you to see the caring leadership, principles, mentoring and problem solving – not to make you an Alcoa metallurgist.

- Alcoa onboarded me – with a real project.
- A solution mattered – reverse "the no aluminum" rule.
- I was not over managed – a command of "strengthen the post" would have constrained me.
- Therefore, I chose to reduce the strength – from 35,000 to 6,000 strength.
- Thus I could gain ductility – improve 5% bend-before-break to 40%.

- I could access competence – a mechanical engineer for rail design.
- I could share and get feedback – at the monthly meeting with my peers.
- I was to report my findings – written, every six weeks.
- When I succeeded – the report went to the big lab in Pittsburgh.
- My boss' boss took it there – he reported to Van Horn monthly.
- My boss debriefed me – authentic caring feedback.
- He gave me learning lessons – so I could grow.
- Others rented the airport – I had no competence for that.
- They crashed the cars – it was fun to see them redirect.
- Others engaged the government – the acceptance was stimulating.
- I told Sally what was happening – she encouraged me.
- Bob Lemon assigned me my next project – for airplane uses.
- Airplanes differ from highway posts – higher strength = more passengers.
- The current alloy was 72,000 strength – invent one 4,000 stronger.
- My new alloy gained the 4,000 – but increased corrosion.
- That project didn't succeed – Bob Lemon mentored me through that.
- I learned on both projects – mentors grow you, not crush you.

- Sally reinforced me too – she loved me, win or lose.
- Both of us benefited – we should raise our children like this.
- God had taught us that – during the Great Depression.
- He can teach you that today – if you will let Him.

Did you see the leadership methods, the principles, the mentoring, amd the constructive and kindly supplied feedbacks that my boss and his boss were giving me? If not, then read the list a second time. Are you doing those when you lead, or when you interface with your child? There are nine more times for you to see those in my positions.

Can you see how very right Professor Wallace's advice had been when he counseled me about the impact of good boss versus bad boss? All of us should choose to be on the good boss path whenever we are the leader.

***

Step 2: Titanium Forgings

Three years later, I was stretched beyond my research roles with aluminum into a broad project that expanded Alcoa past its aluminum roots into the metal titanium. This time, the problem was that the United States government hired Boeing to design and to build a supersonic airplane to transport customers at Mach 2.6 speed (2.6 times faster than the speed of sound). At those speeds, the airplane skin would get so hot that it could no longer be made of aluminum. I was not introduced to the assignment by my boss or my boss's boss.

Instead, Walter Dean, who reported directly to Kent Van Horn, came from Pittsburgh to Cleveland to tell me I was being lent out of my research job. I was to be the metal technology person to learn titanium rapidly so we could build a factory within our existing factory that could produce titanium forgings instead of just aluminum forgings. Two previous efforts had failed for lack of titanium competence. I vividly recall the meeting:

Walter Dean said, This is beyond research. The duration is until we succeed. Your authority will derive from your competence and we will eventually transfer you back into the Alcoa Lab.

Wow, what a stretch. I even had to derive my own way to learn titanium because the Alcoa lab library only covered aluminum. I got rapid learning from Al Favre, the project manager and Bob Bergdahl, the mechanical engineer who built the building and its process machines. Later, when we had product to sell, I paired up with Jerry Hosner, our marketing manager. It worked this time. We immediately set aside our aluminum ways; forcing us to build, operate and sell titanium made the way it prefers to be made.

Fortunately, the principles that Jeffries and Van Horn had discerned applied to all metals and were so robust that I could know both the HOW and WHY titanium had to be manufactured differently from aluminum. A crucial part of titanium metallurgy was that it changed its crystallographic phase (atomic alignment) at a temperature barely above the temperature that was needed for forging. If we didn't heat it hot enough, the metal would crack while the press was shaping it. If we heated it too hot, it would change to a different crystallographic phase, which would impair its mechanical properties. Tightly controlled furnace temperature and quick forging after removal from the furnace were mandatory.

The Alcoa Cleveland plant was a huge aluminum forging plant with giant equipment. The largest forging press was a 50,000-ton hydraulic press, standing five stories above ground and seven stories more below ground; the largest in the United States. By comparison, the hydraulic jack used to lift your car to change a tire is one or two tons. It had a sister press of 35,000 tons, both funded by the government to produce Cold War weaponry. During World War II, this Alcoa plant produced aircraft engines with 13,000 employees, mostly women. The laboratory where I worked was on the corner of the plant. The presses were adaptable for either aluminum or titanium. But virtually none of the auxiliary equipment; such as the furnace to heat the metal for forging, or the heat treatment equipment, could handle titanium.

Our newly assembled team had to change our mental views first. Both of the previous failures were due to aluminum people doing titanium part time, using aluminum principles, methods and viewpoints. There is a learning lesson here because the most seasoned people were so proficient that some aluminum thinking had progressed to autonomous as in the song *"You've got to be carefully taught"* from South Pacific.

Notice the wisdom of Kent Van Horn when he offered a new person to the company for this task, not someone steeped in aluminum. Look at the discernment of Walter Dean when he ignored the normal job title procedure and said:

- Beyond research - he unbounded the domain.
- Until we succeed - success is more crucial than time.
- Competence is first - your authority derives from it.

I was a PhD scientist, and had already been promoted to senior research engineer, yet the best role for me to have on an organization chart would be the one occupied by a fairly new plant metallurgist with a B.S. degree. So I moved into the plant where the action was, set aside any reference to job title, and Walter Dean arranged for my monthly salary to come from the Pittsburgh Alcoa Research lab rather than the plant, for whom I now worked.

I immediately recruited our outstanding librarian Mignon Van Treuren to set up a titanium library and to scan the incoming publications and presentations and to report the titanium trends back to me. Then I visited the companies that would be our customers or our suppliers to get inside the titanium culture, methods, and technologies. I did all of that so that I could help our project leader Al Favre lead and our mechanical engineer Bob Bergdahl build. I was learning from them how to lead and to build.

Aerospace customer examining titanium wing flap forgings with Keith

As we were finishing the building projects and had successfully manufactured some trial titanium forgings, Jerry Hosner, a talented marketing manager, was transferred in from our Los Angeles office. What a bundle of energy! He immediately scheduled meetings with his contacts at Boeing, Lockheed, Grumman, etc. and made me his travel partner. I liked him, but I saw him as a liar. I tried to correct him, but I failed. If something was good, he called it excellent. If it was excellent, he called it fantastic. After a while, I figured out that he was not actually lying. My engineer/science language was too bland for him and the marketer/purchaser language was too exaggerated for me.

But, wow, did I ever learn about customers as people from Jerry. At every visit we made, he would brief me on each person we would contact and what their preferences are. Then, when we left their office, he would debrief me on how I handled each person; kudos for things I did right and kindly mentoring me on how to do better next time (by name, and about what that customer prefers). I really admired Jerry. We successfully gained accreditation for titanium forgings at all of the major aerospace customers.

We booked business to fully operationalize our titanium factory. Along the way, we expanded our metallurgists to four; adding Tom Gurganus, Fred Billman and Bill Kuhlman, three great guys who became highly titanium competent.

I was transferred back into the Alcoa Research Lab but still one hundred percent titanium. Then, after a few months, a huge change occurred; the lab in Cleveland was shut down. Well, almost. They closed the Castings and Forgings division as Alcoa shifted its business away from castings. Many people transferred to the huge lab in Pittsburgh, others into the Cleveland plant, some retired, and a few were laid off. BUT, the titanium business was so important that the lab buildings and organization would remain as a much smaller entity, which I would head.

I was told that I could pick any six people to be part of this lab. Of course, I picked the titanium metallurgists Tom Gurganus and Fred Billman (Bill Kuhlman didn't count as one of the six because he was a permanent employee of the plant). Then I picked Al Montgomery and generated an enormous amount of turmoil because he was my boss.

Al Montgomery on far left

Them - What are you thinking, you can't pick him!

Me - Why not?

Them - Because he's your boss!

Me - So what, he's the best man, so I picked him.

Them - But he can't report to you, and you're the head!

Me - So what, I'll report to him, we know how to work together.

To solve this stalemate, I was called to the Pittsburgh main lab as the human resource people brought in a psychologist to examine me: Why would you do such a thing? Are you turning down your promotion? Are you afraid to lead? Do you feel incompetent? Is there something wrong with your home life? All day long, my answers were "No." Eventually, they and I concluded that I was a peculiar person, more interested in competence and ethics within my newly formed organization than I was in power. I did not adhere to the belief that an organization chart should deny me from working with Al Montgomery.

I was a peculiar person, more interested in competence and ethics within my newly formed organization than I was in power.

Al learned what was happening and immediately took the early retirement option that was one of the choices he had been offered previously. He did not want to hold me back. I chose a replacement for my sixth choice.

I also learned in this early management role what to do when someone who reported to me does things that undermine me or our agenda. It happened, so I asked my mentor. He asked if it was something that had to be addressed immediately. I pondered and then said, "No."

He responded, "If your answer is yes, then you must address it now. However, since you said no, see this as a growth opportunity for both of you. Begin to look for the root cause; the why of the person's behavior. Only then can you lead by solving the right problem in the right way."

I tried what he said. It really worked. All three of us grew.

I'll let you pick the Learning Lessons out of this life story. After you get past the psychology part, look again at each Career/human interaction within the contexts that I've written. God's principles were becoming so deeply imbedded in me that they were shaping my business mantras. I was rarely saying, "This is of God," but my approach to each business situation was godly.

Were you able to look past the metal story and see a learning lesson that you would like to apply to yourself or your child or church group? If so, could you try it today?

***

Step 3: Recycling Aluminum Cans

I had been with Alcoa nine years when I got the call from Bob Spear to head up the innovation team that was being assembled to recycle the aluminum can. I was vaguely aware of the problem but was still totally immersed in titanium.

People had not been very concerned about recycling when Alcoa invested $1 billion in Evansville, Indiana and another $1 billion in Knoxville, Tennessee for factories solely devoted to making the sheet metal from which aluminum cans are made. But now, as environmental concerns increased, the state of Oregon passed a law prohibiting aluminum cans. Their rationale was that the corrosion resistance of aluminum would keep discarded cans as eyesores forever. By contrast, steel cans rusted away and ceased being eyesores.

Alcoa marketing quickly moved into action. Remember now: marketing language exaggerates, and engineering language tends to be cautious. Welcome to round two of that gap. It was not Jerry Hosner this time, but the marketing department immediately launched an advertising campaign titled "YES WE CAN," which claimed that we could recycle cans. Then, to prove their advertising claim, they immediately began buying cans back at an attractive price.

- The ad campaign worked.
- By the time Bob Spear contacted me to solve the recycling problem, Alcoa had bought back 40 million pounds of aluminum cans and was storing all of it in a field; acres and acres of cans fifteen feet high.
- Recall that Jerry didn't lie; he just exaggerated.
- Well, the facts were that it was "possible" to recycle aluminum cans by melting them in the regular-size furnaces that we had.
- But it was very inefficient because one third of the can oxidized away and plugged up the furnace.

So, we "could" and yet, we "couldn't." Such was the problem Bob Spear called on me to engage.

I immediately moved to Pittsburgh to the big lab that had big furnaces where we could engage this problem. Sally remained in Cleveland with five children in the house she had designed. And, oh yes, I left her in charge of another house, the one that we were moving (yes, you read it right, picking up and MOVING it), so that we could make money for the college education of our children. I thereafter used my vacation time every Friday so I could work on the house on an extended weekend and she led the other days. I'll revisit that life story later.

I was promoted to section head within Bob's division and began leading a very talented cluster of people whom Bob assembled out of his division of about fifty people. They quickly brought me up to date with the scope of the problems and the barriers impeding successful recycling. This was not a problem that could be solved within the plant concurrent with their daily production jobs. So we immediately replicated it in the full-size furnace we had in the lab. Sure enough, the problem recurred in all its terrible details. The furnace is the size of a two-car garage and has an open flame at 3400 degrees Fahrenheit blowing just under its roof such that the ceiling temperature is 2700 degrees Fahrenheit. The base is a refractory tub holding one and half feet of liquid aluminum, the temperature of which is 1450 degrees Fahrenheit. Its normal operation would be to add solid pieces of scrap aluminum through the furnace door that would sink and melt.

View from above furnace

Thereafter, the furnace would be tapped (open its drain, just like a bathtub) and the tapped metal would be solidified into a large ingot that would be rolled to a thin sheet for aluminum cans. However, aluminum cans are fluffy, as they hold air here and there, so they float instead of sink, whereupon that intense flame burns then up into a wasteful "hot mess" floating on the liquid aluminum. This was not an easy problem; it was a whole set of hard problems. Multiple people were going to have to solve multiple problems separately, concurrently and connectable. Paul Hess was assigned the search for principles: melt the cans by submerging them in molten salt (not liquid aluminum) so that you can determine which chemical principles are in play. For the full-scale furnace problem, we decided to bring some liquid metal out from under the hot flame: see the drawing of the furnace, its trough and the solutions that worked. The set of solutions required was 12, but the major breakthroughs were two.

Since the problem was that the cans float, it seemed perfectly reasonable to push them under the liquid metal. Wave after wave of submergence methods were conceived of, tested, and even scaled up to production size. The last was a masterful screw feeder that pushed the cans into the liquid aluminum in the trough. But the best and final answer was counterintuitive. Jan Van Linden was a master of stretch ideas and this time, it served us well. He gave up on the word push - a crazy departure! How could you pull from beneath a bath of molten aluminum? His answer – do it like a toilet bowl does. It worked and it is still working 50 years later.

However, a toilet bowl flushes via a torrent of flowing water. That realization triggered the second major invention, this time by Joe Herrick. Steel pumps had been the way to move liquid aluminum from furnace to trough to furnace thus far. They were virtually identical to the sump pumps people use to manage water seepage into basements. They lift water with a rotor turning inside a tube, normally raising a liquid to a foot or two higher. The extent of the lift (how high) is called head and it requires seals to prevent the water from flowing back down. Those design features can work identically with liquid aluminum. But, and this is a HUGE but, liquid aluminum dissolves solid steel. The steel pumps therefore have short lives. Once again, a counterintuitive idea burst forth. As Joe Herrick looked yet again at the trough alongside the furnace, it occurred to him that we didn't need any head at all. Vertical flow was too hard with all the seals and the dissolving, but our need is horizontal, just like it is for boats. Nuts with all that complicated stuff – all that we need is a boat propeller upstream of our toilet bowl. So he made a propeller and shaft out of graphite because it doesn't dissolve in aluminum. The toilet bowl and propellers are still the technology in use fifty years later.

I will cease all this technical description and take you to the consequences.

- We virtually eliminated the oxidation of cans.
- The solution was extremely efficient.
- Marketing could thereby increase our buy-back price.
- Steel cans could not.
- The marketplace chose aluminum, displacing steel.
- Oregon rescinded its "No aluminum" law.

I was intensely proud of my team who had accomplished

this. All of the major breakthroughs were invented by my team, none by me. I gave them the environment for intense and rapid innovation and handled/managed/led the upward interfaces of the company that had to have this solved, wanted it yesterday and frequently let me know it.

The learning lessons were numerous for me and perhaps useful for you. Bob Spear was a great mentor.

Learning Lessons:

- This was really a high-pressure situation.
- Yet we had to be creative, not reclusive.
- Paul Hess' tests revealed the principles by which recycling could work.
- But the pushing, floating, oxidizing and dissolving were hard.
- Innovation can be really high - intense need stimulates it.
- Innovation can be crushed – decrees are harmful.
- An upper manager decreed – "No more funding in Van Linden's area."
- Jan Van Linden pleaded – please let me continue.
- 15% of our budget was solely my choice. – I funded Van Linden.
- The toilet bowl was from that area of inquiry.
- Pressure sometimes leads to rebellion.
- Two engineers blatantly tried to unseat me.
- This one could not wait to look for root causes.

- Confrontation was necessary: "One of us is going to lose and it isn't me."
- "Today is the last day you are going to behave this way."
- He conceded - the entire team was immediately relieved.
- We could recycle every can anyone could ever bring back.
- Marketing had a marketable story, and they loved it.

Did you sense the intensity in this situation? Set aside the cans and their technology and see how the pressures were impacting the people: some decree, some innovate and some revolt. God taught me about this during the Great Depression and War, and now the cans. During those earlier years, we cousins were verbally sharing God's role in all that we were thinking and doing. Since I was now working with Alcoans of other faiths or no faiths, I could not be that open in my discussions. But I could live Godly before them and we could seek and use God's principles. Praying for His guidance and protection was my method to handle this situation. How would you?

Praying for His guidance and protection was my method to handle this situation. How would you?

Alcoa received accolades. The breakthrough was recognized by the United States National Academy of Engineering. They inducted me into NAE and congratulated our team. Shortly thereafter, Bob Spear was promoted to Assistant Director of the Alcoa Research Lab and I was promoted to replace him as Division Manager.

***

Step 4: Manager of Ingot Casting Division

When I became manager of the Ingot Casting Division, I supervised 44 people: 3 administrative assistants, 27 technicians and 14 engineers. We had a very large, well-designed laboratory equipped for small bench scale tests to discern principles, to medium-size scale up for proof of concept and plant-size to prepare for implementation. I walked the floor two or three times every week to know the people and to see their experiments. I usually walked with Lou Resch, our head technician, asking if he thought that this day's progress was generating more than $17,000 of value for the company; the cost of operating our division each day. They were fun discussions. The better I knew each person's talents and skills, the more I could allocate projects based on competencies. My thought was that each person could excel in his or her work and we could therefore have everyone in the top half of our class. I knew that I was distorting mathematics, but person by person, I was seeing motivation and high performance.

When I reached the 43rd person on my staff, I stalled out. My last person was a perpetual talker, which constrained his performance. I simply did not have a position called "chief talker." Then, finally, I saw my opportunity. The person who sorted and delivered mail across the entire campus was going on vacation. So I offered my talker to the administrative department to fill in. I didn't even charge them back for the time he spent there. It worked perfectly; he loved walking and talking all day and the admins liked his performance so much they transferred him.

In that time, General Electric was excelling as a top performing USA company and ascribing their success to their CEO, Jack Welch. Alcoa decided to use some of his management processes such as his method to improve talent: have every manager turn in the names of the bottom 10% performers every year, then fire them and replace them with new higher potential people. Wow, that bore no relationship to the type of person God had grown me to be and the methods I was using in this first job for which my title was Manager. Could the GE method really be imposed on me? Did I have a heart-based model inside of me that was wrong, not tenable in the modern business world? I immediately went to Bob Spear, my Christian boss. He validated me and said he would protect me and my division if Alcoa imposed the GE method. Professor Wallace was right again; reporting to a good boss is precious. I never had to abandon my 44 of 44 agenda – 44 people working in their areas of competence, the company benefitting, their work is fun and people are growing – which is bigger than mentoring. I never had to generate a list of 10% lowest performers.

I will skip writing about the projects of this research division during my first year as manager, only sharing with you that our contributions to Alcoa's business well exceeded our $17,000 per day cost.

Did I have a heart-based model inside of me that was wrong, not tenable in the modern business world?

Once a month, every engineer wrote a three or four sentence summary of that month's status of their projects. The 14 write-ups were then aggregated and sent to every engineer prior to our two-hour monthly meeting. Now, remind yourself that the role of these research engineers and scientists is to solve unsolvable problems. The ones that are solvable are rightly solved in the plants, all of which are staffed with competent employees. So, each engineer at this meeting would share breakthroughs that have occurred or stalemates that are still impenetrable. Peer-to-peer sharing, growth and project enhancement were the objectives. Some projects had already broken through to a solution and, in this meeting, the engineers could get advice on scale-up, thence plant installation.

A second monthly meeting is once again peculiar to the needs of researchers. Without a written agenda or explicit reporting on projects, we met to hear from each other any fresh insights that we have gained that month in concepts, principles, etc. As researchers solving the unsolvable, this meeting's goal was to stretch each other past constraining paradigms. Recall that both major breakthroughs on recycling were counterintuitive. Folks named this meeting "Monthly Miracles." What great examples of team mentoring!

Learning Lessons:

- Managers greatly impact the lives of people.
- The high side uses God's principles,
- Thereby respecting and growing the people.
- Matching talents to tasks is wise management.
- The General Electric approach scares and harms people.
- The winners in GE are stimulated but the losers and also-rans are impaired.
- Bob Spear was simultaneously a manager and a leader of people.
- He passed the two meeting types forward to me to stimulate and to innovate.
- I benefitted from that when he oversaw my leadership during recycling.
- I was learning to manage the division he left. He mentored me.
- Expect disruptions like GE. Insensitivity is commonplace.
- The 44 people went home each night to manage their families.
- My management was intended to build up their home life.
- God's principles rightly applied build up.

- Researchers are peculiar people, perpetually stretching.
- They need to stretch - they are solving unsolvable problems.
- Sometimes such problems occur at home so stretch yourself like these researchers do.
- Your spouse or child may need it - God helps.

I have not mentioned metallurgy or aluminum, concentrating instead on the people, God's principles and God's provisions of talents and gifts. Do you know what He gifted to you? How are you using them? Does your best friend have different talents and gifts? Have you learned to leverage each other with them? Why not try it this week?

***

Step 5: Fabricating Metallurgy and Assistant Director, Research

Jim Dowd, who was assistant director of the lab, became my mentor for my next paired positions, a broadening assignment. I became a potential candidate to become the director of the Alcoa Research Lab. I received a brief lateral move into Manager, Fabricating Metallurgy Division to learn how to manage a different aspect of metallurgy and then I was promoted to assistant director of the lab to lead technologies that were outside the field of my education.

The three divisions assigned to me had connections to aluminum, but not to its metallurgy. The Finishes division covered all of the methods and materials that beautify aluminum with coatings, surface textures, etc. The Engineering Properties division developed procedures and equipment to assess all of the properties relevant to aluminum use like strength, corrosion resistance, ductility and many other potential failure modes. The Design division dealt with the many ways that one can design aluminum to meet functional needs in buildings, cars, etc.

Jim Dowd was now openly sharing with me his assignment to mentor me into broad competence. I also received training in the Alcoa's Advanced Management Programs and in the Harvard Business School summer program for Vice Presidents and Directors of Research and Development organizations. Jim was very thorough in his approach, including how I spoke, how I listened and how I handled conflict. I will skip the technologies of this period, focusing instead on some key learnings I had:

- Nothing I was taught cancelled out the many lessons I had learned regarding God, the Great Depression, War, College, Marriage, Grad school, etc.

- But much was gained in this era during which Jim Dowd broadened me with care and conviction.

- Jim used mock situations to intentionally press me into anger that he video recorded so I could see myself in that situation and correct whatever was revealed.

- Jim put me into intentionally difficult mock management situations and taught me how to handle the heat wisely.

- Jim coached whenever I had a hard situation in real life and during the manager and assistant director positions.
- The Alcoa Management Programs he sent me to were excellent.
- As was the Harvard Business School program led by Renato Tagiuri, globally recognized for his deep understanding of human behavior within each business role (President, Union steward, Foreman, Manager, Research Director, whatever).

Jim Dowd told me when we started this broadening process that he would only have two years to work on me. He was wrong. It was much less than two years for reasons that I will explain after sharing some learning lessons:

Learning Lessons:

- Everyone can gain by constructive broadening.
- Random and painful broadening hurts - it can broaden or repress.
- The constructive broadening is much preferred.
- You can receive it and you can give it.
- Children need it, you can give it - choose the constructive way.
- Constructive is right subject, right way, with caring.
- God's model is the best - it emanates from love.
- Receptivity is crucial - Renato taught us how to be aggressive receivers.

- Don't force the subject when the person is in "low receptivity" (not receiving).
- You will be tempted to press harder with stronger arguments.
- Don't! Both of you will then lose.
- Instead, set the subject aside temporarily and regain receptivity.
- You do that with intensive listening,
- And neutral yet affirming words – "I see this is important to you."
- Or with guttural sounds like: "Oh, Umm, Hmm" with kind tones.
- Receptivity begins with trust. Jim Dowd had earned mine,
- And I had earned his.
- We could move fast and deep and admit if receptivity dropped.
- You can attain trust and receptivity - you can earn them.

Recall my description of children solving problems and discovering the world with their five senses (seeing, touching, hearing, tasting and smelling)? Parents and teachers then discipline that down by the time the child reaches kindergarten. This position required me to re-ignite learning in areas of weakness. It was scary. But Jim Dowd and Renato Tagiuri used God's methods to enhance my receptivity. Do you learn and teach that way? We had progressed very far with Research and Development broadening when the need for business broadening burst onto the scene.

***

Alcoa is a Mature Business – 1980

I was at the Alcoa Technical Center lab the day in 1980 that the Announcement was made. Alcoa had hired a consulting firm to help with our business planning. Their first step was to study the current condition of each of our businesses so the company could have a basis for planning. They had completed their analysis, had reported their findings to Pittsburgh headquarters and then came to the lab to share with us. They reported: ALCOA IS MATURE. That meant that almost all of our business units had passed their peak and were now in a phase where growth was no longer an option. It was as if the air had been suddenly sucked out of the room. We, who were the innovators and initiators of new products and processes, were being told that our industry and company no longer needed our skills throughout the entire core of the company. All 800 of us. I was shocked. We all were shocked.

We, who were the innovators and initiators of new products and processes, were being told that our industry and company no longer needed our skills throughout the entire core of the company.

The consultants continued with their report, advising us that Alcoa should operate our mature businesses, but as cash cows. Don't invest in them anymore, just operate them in such a way that they generate the cash that the company can then use to acquire companies that are earlier in their business cycle, thereby rebuilding the company. The people within our mature businesses reacted similarly to me – heartbroken. "You mean that we are old and now should no longer improve our quality, processes and maintenance? Just cut corners to generate cash for acquisitions?"

The implications of this maturity issue were so harsh that I'll jump ahead to the next two steps, giving you this insight about consequences. Charlie Perry became CEO and later promoted me to vice president. I was saddened for him because he was a kind man and this role was a hard one. He tried valiantly, studied other companies and made acquisitions.

It was hard to make acquisitions and then effectively lead these businesses that you limitedly understand. It also was hard to lead Alcoa core businesses with demotivated people. Charlies' goal was for 50% of Alcoa businesses to be acquisitions.

Learning Lessons:

- Management does not equal leadership,
- No matter how analytically accurate management may be,
- No matter whether it's a corporation, marriage or parent.
- Alcoa was crushed by a single word "MATURE."

- It took seven years to recover.
- God designed us to be relational.
- We surge when relationships are positive and crash when they're negative.
- Crash can be into lethargy or it can be a counterattack.
- Both happened within Alcoa.
- A forklift driver once drove directly at me, then veered off.
- He wanted me to know that he hated his job.
- I would have hated it too.
- This can also happen in a marriage or in parenting.
- So God gave us principles for leading.
- They are explicit in Ephesians, Colossians and I Peter.
- God's leadership principles are for work, marriage and parenting.
- All three rightly done derive from love.
- Ephesians devotes all six chapters to that premise.
- The Alcoa recovery seven years later replaced "mature" with "caring."
- It worked. It really worked.
- Then, much later, the caring ebbed and Alcoa weakened again.
- Read this list a second time. You are a leader in some way.
- Pick the high side. It is a sweet way to travel.

Sometimes major decisions are made that conflict with God's Life Principles. I was grieved when that happened to Alcoa. Then I was transferred into the hot zone of planning these "mature businesses" with these attributes: I had lived this during the Great Depression and Eileen Peretic, my Christian co-worker, heard from God that I was to be like Esther of the Bible, "sent by God for such a time as this" (Esther 4:14). Does God have such an assignment for you?

I was transferred from the lab to Alcoa's corporate headquarters in Pittsburgh to be manager of Business Planning shortly after the MATURE BUSINESS announcement.

***

Step 6: Manager Business Planning

Alcoa's plan to broaden me suddenly moved forward; beyond technologies, Jim Dowd and the Alcoa Research Lab. The next intent was for me to "learn business," so I was transferred into the corporate headquarters in downtown Pittsburgh. I became manager of Business Planning in the Corporate Planning Department reporting to Harry Goern, Vice President of Corporate Planning. Business Planning was an intact department with several seasoned planners who traveled to and helped every business of the company develop and deploy their annual and five-year plans. I knew and liked Harry Goern from previous interactions.

I arrived just before the large intense corporate planning meeting that was offsite for a week in Cape Cod, Massachusetts. Harry immediately put me in front of that crowd. I was to study corporate-wide inventory of aluminum and then to challenge the leaders to reduce it and to locate it strategically. Wow, quite a change from my prior jobs. But I did know how to analyze data and to distill it into findings, so I "did" inventory, presented my findings at the meeting and became known to all the business leaders.

Useful. As soon as I returned from Cape Cod, I began traveling to each of our businesses, paired with the person in my organization who was helping that business.

Within two months, I had an overview of the company; its senior leadership at the Cape Cod meeting, several businesses and their leaders as they developed their plans. I even went to Brazil where we were planning a $1 billion factory in the underdeveloped city of Sao Luis. It was interesting getting to know the CEO, Krome George, and seeing how he was strategizing the company.

But in the exposure to all of this, I detected a gap. The planning process we used in all of our businesses was logical, useful and financial. But it had no method to engage technology. At the corporate planning meeting, I observed that Allen Russell, the vice president of Research and Development, did not have an explicit role in the development of the corporate five-year plan. He was present, well liked and attentive. Yet I, as a newcomer to business, was the one who spoke and challenged the leaders regarding inventory because of its financial impact while the VP of Research was not on the agenda.

I told Harry Goern about my observations. He listened, asked me questions and was genuinely engaged. But he said that I was the fifth person he had transferred into Corporate

Planning from the lab and the very first one to raise this issue. He concluded with "You're very early into this new job so I'd like you to concentrate on learning how to do it well. If, at the end of three months, you still have this concern about technology, come back and tell me again." I obeyed. At the end of three months, I returned, "The gap is even bigger than I first thought." Yet the rigor of the existing planning process worked, was in place worldwide and aggregated up into a consolidated financial plan for the company as a total entity. It was hard to see how to connect technology as it is in an entirely different language than finance. I continued traveling across the nation and around the world, helping all of our businesses develop their business plans.

Don't be surprised that I was seeing God's principles, even though the planning methods were dominantly financial.

***

Step 7: Director Technology Planning

I was then called in to meet with Marv Gantz, Alcoa Director and vice chairman. I had worked with him many years earlier when he was a plant manager within the Cleveland plant where I was working on titanium. His call was to inform me of a decision that the three top technology officers on Alcoa's Board of Directors had made. They were; Krome George (CEO), Edwin Land (a member of Alcoa's board of directors who had invented the Polaroid camera and headed Polaroid Corporation for decades) and Marv Gantz. They had decided that Alcoa must have an organization to do Technology Planning and that I was to head it in a newly created role – Director of Technology Planning. I would work as a separate organization but would work on the same floor of the Alcoa Building as Corporate Planning to be able to collaborate together. They had pre-selected my entire staff – everyone who was in Bob Spear's organization that was doing research planning at the lab (about 12 people). This was no longer the broadening that Jim Dowd had been overseeing. Marv Gantz bluntly stated that Krome, Dr. Land and he did not know HOW to do corporate-wide technology planning, so I would have to both invent and lead it. I immediately knew that the enormity of this role meant that I would never return to the lab to become its director.

I hurriedly went to the lab and met the people who would now leave their research planning jobs and join me in this great new adventure. Then I packed up my wife and five children and departed for Australia and Hawaii for a four-week vacation. It was our 25th wedding anniversary and, since our oldest was 23, we thought it would be the final vacation that all seven of us would take together. We rented a vehicle in Western Australia so my family could see the beautiful mountains alongside which Alcoa had three refineries, worth $1 billion each, and a 90-mile-long ore deposit. We were hosted overnight by Colin Agnew, the plant manager of the Pinjarra plant who had worked with me in Corporate Planning. On the east coast, we flew out to the Great Barrier

Reef in a pontoon plane and overnighted in a sailboat that was permanently anchored above the reef.

Why did I write that paragraph? Because, as usual, God was in charge of our agenda. I thoroughly enjoyed the time with my family but was also impacted by the scenery, the Aboriginal people, the Alcoa host, the kangaroos and the sailboat. God was stretching my mind and my vision. The crowning moment, the place where it all came together, occurred in Hawaii when I stood with my family on the deck of the Arizona, the ship that was not refloated after the bombing of Pearl Harbor.

Left: Attack on Pearl Harbor, Right: USS Arizona memorial

I was saddened for those who died. But I was awestruck by what the survivors had done. Whomsoever they were and howsoever they did it: They immediately refloated, patched and returned to duty 18 of the 21 sunken or damaged ships. Impossible! One would think so. Certainly the Japanese believed that the ships were destroyed or immobilized. But when the Japanese sailed next to attack Midway, another mid-Pacific island, we shocked them. Our patched-together navy and pilots sank all four of the Japanese aircraft carriers. The capacity of people to accomplish the impossible when they are inspired to work together was forever implanted in my brain and heart. We then flew back to Pittsburgh.

The capacity of people to accomplish the impossible when they are inspired to work together was forever implanted in my brain and heart.

The first day I returned to work, I met with the people Marv Gantz had assigned to technology planning. I knew about half of them. I asked about the work they had been doing and learned that it was impressive and that they were very competent. I told them about the important assignment we had and challenged them to conceive of the ways that we could now do corporate-wide Technology Planning; not just research planning and not just business planning, but rather a fresh, connected planning that merged business with technology. We also needed to create it in such a way that it would stimulate people to excel. Everyone joined in and, within a few weeks, we conceived of a technology planning format and tested our methods with businesses as follows:

- Our mantra became "That we may not be steel." There had been about 40 steel mills along the rivers of Pittsburgh, and most were shutting down in 1982.

- We launched the Technology Planning process we had devised for each plant.

- It began with a query – What are the major processes you use to meet customer needs and how have you been improving them regarding attributes, efficiency, and throughput?

- Example: If the customer need is wagons, then ease of pulling is an attribute, prudent use of metal and labor is efficiency and wagons per day is throughput.

- Our target people – about 20 representatives who lead, do, test, enhance or measure these processes.

- We (a pair of us from Technology Planning) then gathered data and plotted graphs like the one below per the query, then called the 20 together and asked how they made those improvements and complimented them for those achievements.

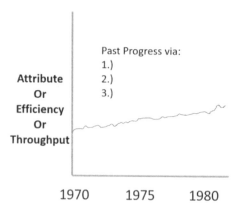

- Then we asked the stretch question, "What is the theoretical limit for your process?"

- The majority of the 20 would not understand the question, but a few who were accustomed to principles would bring up the physics, chemistry or biology that reveal the limit.

- Example: if the query were "how far a golf ball can't travel," some people would discern and say it is governed by club speed plus club head weight plus density of air plus the resiliency of the ball. All four of those answers are correct and derive from physics.

- Do they have to know all four? No. Does everyone have to understand? No. Why? Because the purpose of the questions is to move past mere extrapolation and into the exciting stretch mode that raised the ships in Pearl Harbor.

- The next question draws everyone in. If Jane Doe is right or partially right about those limits, then what ideas do you have that are stimulated by this space between the current performance of your process and this theoretical limit?

- Then, after receiving ideas based upon these inputs, how high might we be able to take the performance of your process? If John Doe offers an answer, then we'd ask if anyone agrees with him? If one other agreed, then we would call that attainment the practical limit.

- The next question would be "How far could we get in one, three or five years depending on which business plan we're attaching this to?"

- The last question would be "What are the enablers you were thinking about when you answered that "How Far" question?" We would record every enabler they offered and create the graph as shown below.

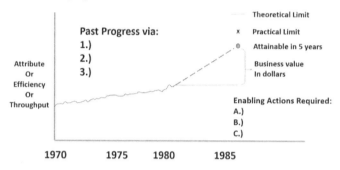

We always had their accountant or finance person in the meeting so they could calculate the financial impact of every "how far" question and feed that into the financial plan of the business.

Alcoa at that time had about 100 locations. We said that we'd cover all of them in two years and then disband. Why choose to disband? Because if we just roared into a business seeking all their process data and asking all of these stretch questions, they might think we were there to displace them and go quiet, the exact opposite of our stretch intent. However, by the time we ended year two, most saw us as helpful, not threatening. They and we were winning the "That we not be steel" goal. It was a little bit like winning the battle at Midway. But the fears associated with MATURE BUSINESSES were constraining our workforce. Then tensions soared when Charlie Perry (the CEO who had replaced Krome George) announced his target for the company to be 50% acquisitions in the next two years.

I added an inspiration beyond the Arizona for ourselves and the people we worked with in all of the businesses. It was the theme song from the Don Quixote movie "Man of La Mancha" as an aged, somewhat crazy old man dressed as a knight in armor who sallied forth to improve the world.

He sang:

To dream the impossible dream
To fight the unbeatable foe
To bear with unbearable sorrows
To run where the brave dare not go
To right the unrightable wrong
To love pure and chaste from afar

To try when your arms are too weary
To reach the unreachable star
This is my quest, to follow that star
No matter how hopeless, no matter how far
To fight for the right, without question or pause
To be willing to march into Hell, for a Heavenly cause

And I know if I'll only be true, to this glorious quest
That my heart will lie peaceful and calm
When I'm laid to my rest
And the world will be better for this
That one man, scorned and covered with sores
Still strove, with his last ounce of courage
To reach the unreachable star

The song in itself is amazing; like the Arizona and "That we not be steel." But the plot of the movie is also stimulating. It is the High Side life story of Aldonza the prostitute, who is the lead woman. Don Quixote sees her at the beginning of the story as a beautiful virtuous woman and by the closing scene, Aldonza has become the virtuous woman Dulcinea that he knew she could become.

God sees the prostitute Aldonza as redeemable into the virtuous Dulcinea. Do you? For a family member, a friend, the person who harmed you? Or even yourself? Might it happen to a Business that is seen as Mature?

I have described in detail the career segment that connected business planning with technology planning because it was a long segment of my career life story (14 of my 40 years) and because it led to three promotions: Director Technology Planning, Vice President Strategic Analysis, and then Executive Vice President Strategic Analysis, Quality and IT. Yet beyond those, there are two more large life stories within those 14 years: a massive mentoring augmentation and a huge high side surge beyond "That we may not be steel."

***

Step 8: Vice President Strategic Analysis

A massive mentoring was initiated by Bob Hornbeck, the new Vice Chairman of Science and Technology, to intensify our learnings from outside the company. From the very onset of our Technology Planning team, we had looked both inside and outside the company. I've already described the inside portion. We did the outside by intentionally looking for companies that were surging past the other companies within their industry or market. Also, we looked at whole industries that were outperforming their competitive industries. In all instances, these surveillances were of interest because they added more stretch to our Technology Planners, and because there could be principles or practices transferrable to Alcoa. We even invented a word for it – transpositioning – meaning that we could lift out the principle behind a gain that was happening in plastics, rework it a bit and then use it to make a gain in aluminum. Bob Hornbeck broadened our search for such ideas by hiring five extremely strong consultants to help us understand global changes in technology and their implications on Alcoa. It was the knowledge aspect of mentoring on steroids. They were our Science and Technology Advisory Council. We visited companies or institutions like Hewlett Packard that were making breakthroughs and we would also visit, assess and help Alcoa plants. We had such visits every month or two for more than a decade. The consultants were picked because they were national experts in technologies linked to businesses:

- Dr. Jay Keyworth: a nuclear physicist who headed the nation's Los Alamos Nuclear Lab and thereafter became the chief scientist of the USA reporting directly to President Ronald Reagan. He led the nation's Star Wars Project to develop defense missiles so advanced and numerous that they would neutralize a nuclear attack by Russia. Star Wars was a key reason that Russia conceded the Cold War.

- Dr. Kim Clark: Dean of Harvard Business School, an economist with strong insights into the impacts of technology on businesses.

- Dr. Kent Bowen: Professor at MIT, leading their Leaders for Manufacturing Program and then Professor at Harvard Business School linking technology to business. Kent led us to Toyota and their powerful system (TPS) that gave them dominance in the auto industry.

- Dr. Robert Mehrabian: a metallurgical engineer who had become president of Carnegie Mellon University. His linkage was metals and business.
- Dr. Ben Streetman: Dean of Engineering at The University of Texas at Austin. He was an electrical engineer with keen insights into the role of technology in all types of businesses.

The two Alcoa members of this Science and Technology Advisory Council were:

- Bob Hornbeck, Vice Chairman Science and Technology (my boss)
- Keith Turnbull, Vice President, Strategic Analysis

L to R: Jay Keyworth, Ben Streetman, Robert Mehrabian, Bob Hornbeck, Keith, Kim Clark and Kent Bowen

Concurrently, we had a very strong Research Lab headed by Pete Bridenbaugh, Vice President Research and Development. It was the lab that had been founded and led by Kent Van Horn decades earlier and was nearly 1,000 strong. We also had a strong Engineering Department with its Vice

President in Alcoa's Pittsburgh Office overseeing engineers, who were within the factories of every Alcoa business.

As I reflect back on this seven-year period from 1979 to 1986, my first thought is that we accomplished the objective "That we not be steel." Steel was hemorrhaging and we were not. We had responded to the MATURE BUSINESS strategy by acquiring some companies and had a goal to reach 50% by the seventh year. The acquired companies had not added great strength to the company so far. Our research lab and engineering organization were still competent. We devised the way to connect technology into our business plans and to identify stretch ideas that could improve businesses.

But we were, as I would describe it, plateaued as a business. From my perspective, the root cause was the shock to our people when they first heard that their careers were starkly at risk. The cause persisted year by year because each acquisition reminded our people that their jobs were at risk. My team of Technology Planners was now seasoned after six years of assisting all businesses. I had been promoted to Vice President Strategic Analysis.

***

Step 9: Paul O'Neill becomes CEO

Seven years after the MATURE BUSINESS announcement, Alcoa's Board of Directors called a private meeting in New York without inviting their chairman, Charlie Perry, and they fired him. They elected Paul O'Neill, who was a recent addition to the board, to become the new CEO of Alcoa. He was at that time president of International Paper Company. He was my new boss' boss.

What a change! His immediate and forever focus was SAFETY; he valued people and was fanatical about keeping all of us safe. Every day generated another story revealing his fixation on the value of the people of Alcoa. His view lined up with the life lesson that there were 37,000 Dulcineas at Alcoa – men and women with undiscovered potential. Because he insisted that every single job had to be safe, he communicated his presence and care to everyone. The company had de-centralized into 20 business units, each with its own president, with a total of 17 different email systems. Paul did not let that impair his safety initiative so he mandated that every president send him a business status report every Friday on Paul's email that he would respond to every Monday via his email to theirs. That new connectivity required every injury or near miss be reported to him immediately. All 37,000 Alcoans knew immediately that they had a new Boss and that this one boldly declared and demonstrated that YOU MATTER TO ME.

Paul was safety focused, but not narrowly caring. When it was time to renew Alcoa's membership in a country club where our marketing department brought customers, he asked "Do they conform to our ethics? Is it integrated?" The answer was no, so he refused to renew unless Ernie Edwards, our African American treasurer, could become a member. The country club removed its barrier and we renewed our membership. Our people worldwide embraced their new environment and blew right past "That we not be steel" into the high side like when Pearl Harbor refloated ships and Don Quixiote sang to *Dream the Impossible Dream*. He brought no one into Alcoa with him and he fired no one. He totally ignored the report that said we were MATURE. Within a few months, he shared his thesis:

- Control – every business is in an industry and is impacted by its industry. However, more than 50% of the factors determining success are within the control of the people within that business and that is enough to excel.

- Best – every industry has a business that is performing best and that business is a very successful business.

- Aspire – I have now seen our businesses and saw evidence that we are not yet best. I challenge you to commit to be best because I know that you can.

- Timing – you are secure in your job and accountable. I will help you in whatever ways I can so that we can accomplish these improvements in three years.

The cloud was lifted. The Mature Business consultants were right about our calendar maturity but were wrong about our people maturity. When Paul saw the strategic analysis data we had collected and the improvement paths that had been revealed, he embraced them and immediately intensified their attainment. He was educated as an economist, but he declared finance to be the secondary language and measure of business success, with non-financials being the primary. Every business has customers with needs and processes to meet their needs. Therefore, every business must first clearly determine the customer needs, and then use their strategic analysis findings so that their people can effectively use their processes to meet these needs. Those plans must be presented by each business unit president to Paul as their non-financial plan before he would review their financial plan.

We doubled in employment, tripled in revenues and quadrupled in profit and market cap (the stock market value of the company). Our core company became strong and vital. Acquisitions to replace core businesses ceased, but several acquisitions that were additive to the core company capabilities were made.

Alcoa 1980-2003 Dollars in Millions				
Year	Revenue	Earnings	Market Cap	Employees
1980	$5,148	470	4,121	
1981	4,978	296	4,944	
1982	4,648	11	6,566	
1983	5,263	174	4,889	
1984	5,751	256	5,477	
1985	5,163	(17)	6,140	
1986	6,431	254	6,130	
1987	7,767	200	7,740	55,000	O'Neill arrives
1988	9,795	861	9,257	59,000
1989	10,910	945	11,016	60,600
1990	10,710	295	11,842	63,700
1991	9,884	63	13,662	65,600
1992	9,492	(1,139)	30,523	63,600
1993	9,056	5	28,995	63,400
1994	9,904	375	30,132	61,700
1995	12,500	791	19,245	72,000
1996	13,061	515	33,003	76,800
1997	13,319	805	27,366	81,600
1998	15,340	853	25,734	103,500
1999	16,323	1,054	26,041	107,700
2000	22,936	1,484	30,242	142,000
2001	22,859	908	9,012	129,000	O'Neill leaves
2002	20,263	420	15,707	127,000
2003	21,504 (tripled)	938 (quadrupled)	15,729 (quadrupled)	120,000 (doubled)
*Source – Jim Hagedorn via Bloomberg Annual Report				

All Alcoa businesses became SAFE and strong. Our safety performance surged into the ranks of the safest companies in the world. Every process had safety procedures that underwent continuous improvement. Every injury or near miss was investigated to find ways to prevent its recurrence. Everyone helped; the objective was improvement, not punishment. However, when two nuns attended our annual shareholders meeting and reported that our Mexican plant in their city was "covering up" a breach in safety, Paul immediately dispatched two vice presidents to investigate. There was a cover up and the business unit president knew, but did not act. He was fired immediately – he had breached Alcoa's ethics.

Every business embraced Paul's four points for their improvement; Control, Best, Aspire, Timing. They were stimulating and deployable just like safety had become. At every Friday email, every business shared progress with Paul and received his feedback on Monday. Many business unit leaders believed the reports should be private, but not Paul. He believed that every Alcoan should hear about the progress that their work was causing.

Seven years after Paul became CEO, he launched a second initiative called "Closing the Gap – We Can Do It," and made officer-level changes. I was promoted to Executive Vice President, gained two more assignments (Quality and IT) and became a member of Paul's eight-person Executive Council.

The information intent, methods, hardware and software needed to undergo extensive change. We had a centralized mainframe, but with 17 different email systems. Much scrambling and patching was necessary to comply with the requirement for the Friday and Monday reports. Paul and our Science and Technology Advisory Council arranged for the requisite upgrade help to come via collaboration with Lewis Platt, CEO of Hewlett Packard.

The purpose for acquisitions was reversed: buy the businesses that strengthen our core, not the ones that replace it. Therefore, when the Iron Curtain came down and Hungary became a free nation, its aluminum manufacturing became an orphan, no longer integrated with plants within USSR and unskilled in marketing as communism doesn't market. Therefore, we bought the entire Hungarian aluminum business, operated it, grew it, added jobs and paid taxes – quite an improvement for the Hungarian government that had been losing money in their aluminum business and taxing its people to cover the losses. We thereafter purchased the Italian and Spanish government-owned aluminum factories. In any such acquisition, Paul was the final voice in the buy/don't buy decision, always ensuring that the candidate acquisition met this revised intent and was likely to succeed.

I could go on with enough of these stories to fill another complete book because I worked alongside Paul O'Neill for 14 years. But I will stop because by now you know that he was a Godsend for Alcoa.

***

Step 10: Toyota's System

My 10th position was to learn the Toyota Production System (TPS) and implement it companywide. It is an incredible system; birthed as a production system then expanded into an enterprise-wide system. The system is 75 years old but some key elements were in place 100 years ago, during the Roaring Twenties. It can be applied to almost any human endeavor.

For the purpose of this book, I will not attempt to teach you the system, choosing instead to show some elements potentially useful for your life story. Its beneficiaries are its customers and its people. Its nemesis – the reason it is so rarely deployed successfully outside of Toyota – is command and control management behavior. I was trained by Hajime Ohba, one of the top 12 TPS experts in Toyota. He was sent to America to develop local suppliers of parts for Toyota cars and trucks built in the USA, Canada and Mexico. We implemented TPS worldwide in Alcoa. It was highly successful in some plants and businesses, but failed to convert the whole company system. My last assignment before retirement was to write a book on what TPS is and how to do it. The book's title is *The Alcoa Business System.*

I can pass its pieces forward to you to use in your life story as Learning Lessons, starting with the ones that are easiest to understand and to deploy.

CUSTOMERS:

1. Customer satisfaction is high – when you meet customer needs.

2. Customers may not know needs – you can help them know.

3. It is good to know customer wants – sometimes you should meet wants.

4. Wisdom is necessary for 1 to 3 – it guides your sorting of need/want.

5. Oversupply and undersupply are wrong – both are wasteful and misleading.

6. The "Just in time" principle is right five ways – quantity / type / time / to / from.

7. Toyota masters item six – people wrongly think "just in time" means inventory.

8. Weakness in any of these seven is bad – it causes waste, distrust and rework.

9. All seven are common sense – requiring attitude, caring and doing.

10. They apply broadly – to a child, spouse, church and you.

PEOPLE:

Toyota really values people and so might you.

11. "People are our most valuable resource" – Toyota REALLY means it.

12. People have an innate desire to improve – Toyota fosters it.

13. People have unlimited capability to learn – life long.

14. People use their senses to excel – seeing, hearing, feeling, smelling, tasting.

15. Processes, machines and materials – must communicate to those senses.

16. There is a name for such communication – Built-In Tests.

17. Built-In Tests enable the human to thereby concurrently - Do/Inspect/Improve.

18. Examples: Hands feel the Doing, Eyes see Inspection, Brain thereby improves Work.

19. People are our most valuable resource – they do all three concurrently.

20. People who are doing all three – are motivated and successful.

Notice how the three done concurrently – Do/Inspect/Improve - is God's High Side of human activity from infant up unless it is repressed by bosses, parents, et al, managing by Command and Control.

PROBLEMS:

21. But problems happen – they are good. You are good.

22. Solve problems close in time, place and person to occurrence,

23. Assisted by a nearby mentor – who begins with What, not Who.

24. Together they diagnose – to root cause, not just symptoms.

25. Both grow via problem solving – rightly done.

26. The mentor thanks and compliments – her most valuable resource.

27. Improvements are conceived – by the person or mentor.

28. They conceive of a way to test it – ideally the same day.

29. If it works, they celebrate – brains are precious.

30. If it didn't work, discern why – was it a problem, cause or solution?

31. Think of a way to test it – by tomorrow, if you can.

***

Everything you have just read is doable with your child, your spouse or your next door neighbors. Why don't you try it? Pick one line, or two or three lines that intrigue you. Then do it now. Toyota does, I do, and my son does.

<u>BUT – COMMAND AND CONTROL DOES NOT</u>

The reasons not to do it are legion. Too bad. Businesses, hospitals and others like them see it as giving too much authority to the doer and thereby threaten their legacy, its management systems, techniques and measures.

Let's pick a real example to see how to do it. Lines 14, 15 and 16 are a good place to start. Let's presume you are driving a car, then your seeing, hearing, feeling and smelling are your <u>receivers</u> of information (taste is highly unlikely). The <u>senders</u> of information to you are *seeing* (windows, backup camera and gauges in the dashboard), *hearing* (seat belt not fastened and a few others), *feeling* (no intentional feedback but the car vibrates sometimes), and *smell* (overheating causes smells).

These and other sensors, systems, etc. are input into a computer that turns on a yellow light that informs you to Check Engine. This is BAD COMMUNICATION. It says worry, but it won't tell you why. It implies actions, but it doesn't tell you which. It ignores timing (now, later, or whenever) but doesn't tell you what you actually need.

It has a lot of engineering cleverness, wiring harness integration (100 wires in the dashboard alone) and computer programs that have increased the sticker price and underserved the driver. The preferred approach is BINARY: Clear, Accurate, Concise and Sufficient such that it meets the customer need. The second communication attribute is DIRECT from its sending source to the driver, now, while she is driving, with the actions she must now take so that she is safe and the car is minimally impaired by the problem.

Now let's make all of that simpler. How do you communicate with your two-year-old child, your 10-year-old, 17-year-old, spouse, neighbor, coworker, you name it? You can begin the assessment by listening to yourself, then asking your spouse to listen. Then you can ask yourself "How am I teaching my children to communicate?" Then there are the infrastructure questions: "How is your life story thus far making it easy for love to flourish, or constraining it because of past hurts not yet reconciled?" As usual, the best way to handle these improvement opportunities is to look at God's principles and then do as He has prescribed.

After you use 14, 15 and 16 as effective Learning Lessons, let your spouse or daughter pick a line or so from the remaining and see how a second such query can enhance your life story. Using elements of TPS in this way can be helpful.

***

Career Story – A Reflection

I have shared the 10 steps of my Career with you because they are integral to our life story that Sally and I promised to write with honesty and candor. With that intent, how would I summarize the Career part of our story that you have just read?

First, I must say that Sally, my children and God were crucial enablers. Sally supported me as a wise and caring partner who saw the significance of each Career step and then joined with me as we sought to see God's intent. She then constructively bridged the life changes the Career caused for our family and her. One example would be increased weekday travel required for the titanium launch, then the move to Pittsburgh for can recycling, followed by the global travel for the latter 20 of my 40-year career. Weekends were precious for all of us: 100% dedicated to God and Family. Our love never wavered.

The second Career summary was that my intent was always to travel God's Kingdom road that He prepared for me, not to become an executive vice president. However, Eileen Peretic was right when she heard from God that I had an Esther assignment: "Who knows but that you have come to a royal position for such a time as this." I was the tagalong nurtured by older cousins during the Great Depression, and the wanderer in the wilderness for my entire senior high school dating career. Why? So I could be prepared to lead from my heart, as I was increasingly engaged in the more crucial decisions within Alcoa. I was God's ambassador with the knowledge that His principles applied everywhere every time.

The third Career summary was, WOW, was it ever an amazing Career life story in the ways that business people keep score. We did not crash the way the steel industry did. We were wounded but not broken by the MATURE BUSINESS era. Then, we surged forward during the 14-year Paul O'Neill era. I was a scientist whose business training was selling a few dogs in a pet shop where I cleaned kennels. Did I need mentoring? You bet! Did I receive it? Perpetually, by skillful, caring mentors.

Yet in all of those huge changes, I was and am a product of the cousin experience during the depression/death/stroke era. I was the youngest of seven, the tagalong, not the leader, but I was A COUSIN with full stature as my mother and aunt closed ranks and led us through very difficult times. I learned not to run away from hard things nor to become depressed, but to close ranks, to collaborate and to trust God.

How Did I Learn These Jobs?

I had 10 positions during my 40-year Alcoa career that delivered value to the corporation such that I was "earning my keep," a colloquial expression that meant the value of my work was greater than my salary. My early positions were metallurgically intense, meaning that the value derived from my years of education that taught me the engineering of metals and the science of metals. But, by the fourth position, my value was based upon "Managing" - something not taught in my nine years of college. Then, by the sixth position, my value was "Business," again not taught. The seventh position was "Invent it" – we can't tell you how. The eighth was "Global Motivation of 37,000 Alcoans" via strategic analysis, the invention that we devised in step seven. The ninth was "Corporate Leadership" within the Alcoa CEO's Executive Council. The tenth was to "Learn and Deploy the Toyota Production System" into all Alcoa businesses. Read that paragraph again yourself the question: HOW DID KEITH LEARN THOSE JOBS?

The answer to that question is the people who mentored me. What wisdom they didn't know, they sent me out to learn in short courses or brought experts in like the Science and Technology Advisory Council. They also challenged me to "Invent it" as in Position 7. Notice that Position 10 is 100% mentored from outside the company.

I was mentored intensely and I, in turn, mentored the people who reported to me. That carried over into my family and can to yours as well. We all have a choice with regards to mentorship and it works best when you take it to the high side with both "what" and "how." God is the author of this and the Bible is His written manual.

11

Family Formation

Now that we have finished the 40-year, 10-position and many-principled Career life story, it is time to return to the God/Family story that was concurrent with those 40 years. Recall that we had previously taken marriage, our foundation, principles, mentoring and problem solving to the high side. Thereafter, as we focused on Alcoa, we have brought career to the high side as well. All of those were attained by using God's principles.

Let's therefore consider the profusion of principles poised to impact Family in this God/Family four decades and beyond. We were becoming mother, father and five children surrounded by principles.

There are Principles that were put in place by God as the

ways He designed and operates the universe. The other Principles are God's Life Principles that He put in place as guidelines for us that are derived from His love, grace, mercy and imparted hope. Because we have free will, many people believe there is no God, search for alternative genesis models for all of the universe principles, and devise their own personal view of morals and ethics. Sally and I believe there is a God, precisely as He describes Himself in the Bible, who has principles of the universe that function whether we know what they are or not. Two of those were discovered within 300 meters of each other where I went to college (crystallinity of metals and the first measurement of the speed of light). God treated His principles for human behavior quite differently than the universe set. He wrote them all in the Bible that explains them, repeats them and implores us to use them. However, because we have free will, we use some, ignore others, reinterpret them, etc., thereby missing their merit.

The ways we lived the life story of our family are the sincere but imperfect ways we tried to obey God's principles as our foundation and guiding light. Please recall that our two-point yearning once we fell in love was Marriage and Family. Not the careers we were studying to attain. Not wealth. Not power. Not prestige. We just flat out loved each other and yearned to have children to love.

We thank God for the five children He blessed us with. We love them and they love us back. Immediately, we engaged them into our church, its activities and its many ways of nurturing children. Pastor Doug Couch and his wife Sally loved our children as did our cousins, the ones we bonded with during the Great Depression. Bruce and Marilyn Clark, the family that alerted us to the importance of right parenting, were also important. My aunt Dorothy, the widow who teamed with my mother in the depression/death/stroke days, sold in 1965 the 10-acre family farm she had inherited to the church for a low price. This enabled our church to build a new church building and to move out of the school that we had rented for Sunday services. I was chairman of the church building committee at the same time that we were building a titanium plant at work and Sally and I were building a new home in Cleveland.

So what did we do with our children? We onboarded them. Not at Alcoa, they of course wouldn't let them. But, at the church and at our new home, we engaged them in the work at hand, even June at age 1 ½ (Jim wasn't born yet). We made work fun and fulfilling. Some very young raccoons joined into the house building process. They were so friendly that they would even climb up our legs. The daytime

Baby raccoons in 1963

carpenter found that less appealing than our kids, so he moved the raccoons 10 miles away when he went home one day.

Our builder was a member of our church, a third generation builder/carpenter. His father built Sally's parents' house back in the Roaring Twenties. He coached Sally as the two of them designed our child-friendly home. He knew and loved our kids so he left them kid-friendly tasks to do at the house every evening. He only built one house at a time and was on site every building day so the project, and the learnings, were conflict free. Our children really liked this kind man.

But the house wasn't the agenda – it was the means that supported Sally's leadership as a mentor of children. The two-child family model that her parents had and expected her to also have was hugely expanded to include our kids (a mob of five), our neighbor's kids, church kids and whoever. Our backyard in Cleveland abutted the huge Metropolitan Park and we owned the trail that went down 100 feet to the Rocky River as it was flowing toward Lake Erie. It attracted kids and Sally welcomed them. That model continued and expanded further when we later moved to Pittsburgh and bought the seven-acre Campbell Lake for our backyard.

What I have just described took place while I was working on titanium forgings in Cleveland. I was actively involved in all this while being keenly aware that my love for Sally should support her totally as God was growing her into the person He intended (Ephesians 5:25-28).

"Husbands, love your wives, just as Christ loved the church and gave himself up to her to make her holy, cleansing her by the washing with water through the word, and to present her to himself as a radiant church, without stain or wrinkle or any other blemish, but holy and blameless. In this same way, husbands ought to love their wives as their own bodies. He who loves his wife loves himself."

That Ephesians 5 Principle was our guiding light, for both our construction process and Sally's extensive engagement with grade school girls in our church's Pioneer Girl bible-based program.

Family and Friends

From the very moment we fell in love, we yearned for Marriage and Family. Three years later, we married and were thrilled by it for the two years leading up to our first child. We were still in Cleveland near both sets of parents and our beloved cousins from Great Depression days. We also had good friends from college, school and neighborhood. But marriage changed dynamics and children were poised to bring a second, yet greater change.

We had a friend Jim Norton who owned a water ski boat that was great for guy trips to western Lake Erie. We were frugal since none of us had much money. But, as we and our buddies became mixed - single, engaged or married - our trips didn't quite work anymore.

From left Ken Turnbull, friend Larry Toriello and Keith
Right: Jim Norton

We tried one trip where people slept in cars, separated by gender. That didn't work; it was too hot to keep the windows closed, and mosquitos invaded if we opened the windows. We tried a second time by renting a few motel rooms for all of the girls while the guys slept in and around the boat and its trailer. The gals liked it but we guys suffered from the wind and rain and then couldn't go water skiing in the morning because the lake was too choppy.

Then we began having children and those types of trips became ancient history. So we morphed into enclosed space, with mosquito net windows, and baby provisions including porta cribs inside. It was serious tent camping. Now 62 years later, that still is the predominant way our 55-person family and many assorted friends vacation each summer.

I shared those two stories to make perfectly clear the principle: that Single and Married and Parent are NOT the same. These three differ so much that a person who changes to a next phase may well lose the comraderies and friendships of people who did not advance now or perhaps never will. However, we absolutely did not want our transition to Married and then Parents to impair our friendships.

That risk is what led the Turnbull family and our friends to Kelley's Island, our most preferred place to vacation.

When we first discovered this campground, its rating was primitive, its toilets were outhouses, its water was a faucet in the middle of the campground, and its showers were nonexistent. That meant bathing in the lake after dark with Ivory soap because it floats. Furthermore, you had to take a ferry boat to get to the campground. But it was child friendly and that trumped the impositions. Why? Because parents can camp on the beach, which is a HUGE advantage when a family has two or more children. The infant can sleep in the tent while the older siblings play in the lake. Kelley's Island was the only campground in Ohio with that amenity that is so very precious for mothers and fathers of young children. It liberates the parents to fellowship easily with our single and married-without-children friends. Ohio has subsequently modernized the campground with showers, electricity and playgrounds. How does this fit into the agendas of the single person and those married-without-children? Easily, because the major activities of swimming, boating, water volleyball and tubing are right outside the tent where an infant is sleeping. How does this affect relationships during times beyond vacations? Greatly. It focuses adult leaders like Sally to meet both child and parent needs in ministries like Pioneer Girls, Children's Ministry, and the trail to the park below our Cleveland house. It also serves as the means to handle whomsoever comes to our lake to get invigorating relief from the isolation of COVID-19 in 2020.

Sally and I transitioned from single to married to parent joyfully and we retained our friendships with the singles and the married-without-children friends. We were diligently seeking and finding God's ways to transition into the high side of both of our aspirations: Marriage and Family. Sharing became a norm; at Kelley's Island with food, cooking, boats and bikes; and also at home with toys, chores, agendas and repairs.

A strange thing happened as we increased our children from one, to two, to more. When Sally would leave our firstborn with me for a few hours, Ken would totally occupy my time; so also when I was to care for both Ken and Steve. But when the numbers increased to three, four and five, they occupied less and less of my time, down to about 25%. Why? Because they were increasingly working or playing with each other such that my role was shifting from participant to team coach.

Sally and I made the decision and explained to our children that we would not treat them equally because they were such different children. But we would always seek to treat them fairly. Sally and I would define "fair" and would welcome their input if they thought we erred on any decision.

In all that you have just read, we have been replicating the love-linked life style of the "COUSINS" during the Great Depression, but without the nationwide trauma that was present when we were the age of our children. God was our provider and protector. We perpetually sought to follow Bruce Clark's advice. The instruction book is the Bible, leading us to the high side of family and we loved it and them.

We loved our neighbors: Cy and Mary Bliss and their four children; Jim and Pat Russell and their three children; our single friend Ralph Garlick, and the not-so-near neighbors like my cousins. Pat and Jim didn't go to church so we took their three children with us to church every Sunday.

My mother died shortly after our third child was born in 1963. She was a woman who bestowed love upon others so the funeral procession was nearly 300 cars long. God blessed me with 26 years of love-based mentoring by a "love thy neighbor" expert. How fortunate it was that she and physically-crippled Martha graduated to heaven two hours apart. How reassuring it was to watch Sally rise up into the role of motherhood as the apprentice, now the master. My mother's persistent prayer for me was answered the day I stopped going steady with Jane Doe and chose Sally as my wife-to-be. Thus was the life story God was overseeing as He transitioned Sally and me from teenagers to parents. Thank you God for coaching Kent Van Horn and Jack Wallace to keep us in Cleveland with cousins and parents during the decade we formed our own family.

As we completed our first decade of Family Formation, Sally reported on them in our 1970 Christmas letter.

Christmas 1970

Jim, our youngest at 2 ½, is into the "terrible twos" and making Sally wonder how she ever lived through this stage with the others. He has at two different times decorated our walls with magic marker and sprinkled cleansing powder and bath soap powder all around the house – including all over our brown miniature poodle, Pepper! Most recently, we found Jim clinging tearfully ¾ of the way up our back hillside (shale cliff) unable to climb either up or down. We still don't know if he fell over from the top or climbed up from the bottom – but either thought gave us a few more grey hairs that we don't really need.

June, 6, graduated from nursery school into kindergarten this fall. She went to Safety Town during the summer to learn all about getting to and from school carefully, as she rides her bike daily with the older 3. She and Jim go ice skating when Sally teaches pre-school learn-to-skate classes, and June also has figure skating lessons. Since starting school, she has really blossomed into a little lady for us – wonder of wonders!

Lynne, 8, is a 2nd grader who is terribly excited over anything and everything she does in life – Brownies, Bible School, piano lessons, Sunday School, figure skating, swimming and school. This past winter she even won a nice trophy at the Silver Skates races just before coming down with chicken pox with 3 others in the family.

Steve, 9, is in 4th grade, and is banking his paper route money so some day he can become a "Meddler" like his Dad.

(Metallurgist is still a big word for him.) Steve and Ken, only a year apart in school, share many of the same activities; baseball sessions in the spring, hockey in the winter, Christian Service Brigade and airplane classes sponsored through our church, and piano lessons.

Ken, 11, is a 5th grader who did more traveling this year than any of our family (with the exception of Keith). Because of his excellent route collections, he won a 5-day all-expenses paid trip to Disneyland in California during June. He had barely returned from that fabulous trip when he went off to Camp Patmos (our church camp) on Kelley's Island for a week of fun and spiritual growth.

Our children are bubbling with excitement at the moment over what they consider Pepper's personal Christmas gift to them – 5 darling pups (just right for 5 kids, huh!) – which arrived as we were writing this missive. The best part was that the 4 oldest children all watched the miracles of the pups' birth and how Pepper so instinctively and ably handled the whole matter, start to finish.

Although Sally played volleyball last spring, she found her schedule too taxing to play again this fall, what with Bible studies, teaching ice skating, typing for the church, acting as a guide for Pioneer Girls (the girls' counterpart of Christian Boys Brigade, similar to Girl Scouts), and trying to oversee the family's activities.

The learning lessons for us were numerous during this period of family formation, and we trust that some will be useful in your life story.

Learning Lessons – the First Decade of Family

- Children are a gift from God – never forget it.

- Raising them God's way – is the best way.

- Love for them comes immediately – God designed us that way.

- Children test our love – free will has that downside.

- The first child matters – they change everything.

- Parents adjust to the change – it is an imperative.

- Love enables the change – otherwise parents would crash.

- A second child seals the change – family becomes your essence.

- Children are intensely active – love that or you will suffer.

- Child activity can be fun – if you join into it with them.

- Work can be fun – if you engage them properly.

- Children need feedback – compliment them as they learn.

- Children need discovery – parents can design work that way.

- Children need discipline – to learn right from wrong.

- Discipline must not be abusive – but it must have consequences.

- At third child, family becomes a crowd – they're the majority.

- Four children in five years is fast – fortunately they liked each other.

- At fifth child, family is a mob – for the better or the worse.

- God was important in this – for the 1st, 2nd, 3rd, 4th and 5th.

- He imbedded love in all five – parents must nurture that love.
- Growing that love is a thing of beauty – don't crush it.
- God will mentor you as a parent – be sure to let him.
- God will use the hard times – if you will let him.
- Hard times will grow us – don't let them crush you.
- We love our children – always will.
- Their faith in God – is our greatest blessing.
- Friends and relatives matter – they influence your family.
- Children of other families matter – they influence your family.
- Kindness in those relationships matter – your children learn kindness.
- Church is a great place for children – God, love and friendship.
- So are right kinds of outreach – Fifth grade girls were Sally's favorite.
- Camping is great for children – It feeds their discovery intent.
- Animals are a part of camping – but raccoons don't belong in tents.
- Campfires are great for meals – and devotions before bedtime.
- Children can lead devotions – sharing life stories with siblings.

Living in Two Cities

In August 1971, I was transferred to the big lab, Alcoa Technical Center in Pittsburgh, to develop the technology for recycling aluminum cans. I moved to my Pittsburgh job immediately, leaving Sally and our children in Cleveland. There were two reasons for their delayed departure: we needed a Pittsburgh house and we were moving a Cleveland house. You read that correctly: we were lifting up a house and moving it to a new location. Shortly before my transfer, Sally and I decided to buy a house that was in the way of Interstate 480 highway construction and planned to move it to earn money for our children's college education. But then, Bob Rogers, the cousin who rose up to be the substitute father of the cousins during the Great Depression, visited us and had a heart attack. He and his wife were missionaries with five children and very little money. Sally and I quickly realized that God's purpose for the house was for this family, not for the college education of our children. We shared that conviction with our cousins and our church, and the entire move-the-house to move-the-Rogers family-in was completed in three months with 100% volunteer labor except for the equipment-intense lift up and set down. Bob recovered and moved into his house with his family in December.

The government bought the house for $45,000. We bought it from them for $1,625, moved it for $5,000 and built out the new basement into bedroom space for $10,000 in materials.

I share this because it almost had a huge impact on our Pittsburgh living. I used my vacation days on Fridays so that I had extended weekends to work on the basement rebuild, etc. for the moved house. Then Sally led the project Monday to Thursday. As I departed Cleveland on a Sunday evening in November, I told Sally to make sure the volunteer with the backhoe would dig the sewer trench on Monday because he was planning to leave our project and we must complete the move-in before winter stalls the project.

Sally arrived early Monday morning, a cold rainy day. The only other person who came was the backhoe man to load up and leave. Sally said "You can't, we have to put in the sewer today." He responded "Who is the who? No one came." Sally replied, "I am the who. You dig and I'll lay the sewer." I called her the next day to tell her I found a lake in Pittsburgh where we could build a house. Her response was "Absolutely not. I got so cold putting in that sewer yesterday that I NEVER want to build a house again." That settled that!

We looked at houses to buy from then until February. Then, finally, Sally forgot how cold she had been that frigid day in November and relented enough to say "Ok, let's buy the lake and build our house, but do it in warm weather." God had ministry intents for the house and lake that we had never anticipated. Once again, He was guiding us past mere housing to His high side of mentoring space.

We bought the lake and, while I was working in Pittsburgh, Sally met with our prior builder in Cleveland to replicate and upgrade our house. Using photos and surveys, they designed to fill in the low land behind the lake's dam and to have the house service the lake like a beach house for summer water sports and a warming house for winter sports. Ingress, egress, dirty shoes, apparel change, skate change and bathroom access were all designed in. Those led to the extended family room, enlarged garage and an added bedroom for Jim, who was born after our Cleveland house was built. We bid the drawings and specifications with local contractors and awarded the construction contract to Adolph Kokoscenski. We retained all of the finishing, grading and landscaping portions for our family to do.

Family Enrichment

I moved to my new recycling of cans job in August 1971. Sally describes her perspective of our move in our 1972 Christmas letter as follows:

December 1972

For those of you accustomed to transfer, we're sure you'll get a chuckle to learn that we completed our transfer to Pittsburgh in a mere 14 months. Three months of house hunting convinced us to build again. The remaining eleven months slipped by as our real estate purchase became entangled with sewer assessment problems, hurricane Agnes converted our newly dug basement into Lake Mudhole, and a spurt in building activity brought on a shortage of tradesmen and material. Home port throughout the time was our Cleveland home. Keith commuted weekends through September, at

which time an "on time" school and a "behind schedule"
construction project expanded the commuter rolls to 1 dog, 5
exasperated scholars and 2 beleaguered parents. We were
extremely fortunate to find a couple willing to rent us a 4-room
duplex. It was small, by comparison, but most adequate in
almost every respect, even to including a special bonus feature
which the kids really enjoyed – unlimited use of the owner's
pony, Ginger.

Thanksgiving week, we moved into our new home, moved out of our rental, and turned over the Cleveland home to its new owners. Our new setting is more "country" than Rocky River and the river that had been our Cleveland backyard has been replaced by a seven-acre lake. The children have already enjoyed water skiing on it and are now anticipating the ice-skating season.

We built our house upon the low land behind the dam such that our first floor matched the elevations of the dam crest and our basement floor was 10 feet lower than the dam crest, as you can see in the photo from behind the dam.

It took two years of living with mud to get enough fill dirt so that we could walk on level land the 80 feet from our first-floor door to the dam. Yet our children loved it. They used pallets and whatever for a crude walkway to the lake where they had a raft (no dock yet) so they could enjoy the lake, swimming in warm weather and ice skating in cold.

On left, Keith standing in the future home's basement, with the dam 4 feet higher than his head. On right, enjoying ice time.

This time, our children are seven years older than when we built our prior house so as soon as we moved into our three-month rental house, they rapidly and effectively did all of the internal finishing (painting, etc.) and the external (landscaping and grass). In the rental home, there was one living room where all of the children slept. We had small suitcases with our clothes and sleeping bags and pillows to sleep on the floor. There was no dishwasher, so we had to do all of our own dishes at the rental home. The one sore point in building our new home was removing rocks from the free fill dirt that became our front yard – a hard and tedious job by wheelbarrow.

When we first moved from Cleveland to Pittsburgh, we searched for a new church to "grow up" in. We didn't immediately find one nearby, so Sally got a list of all of the Pittsburgh churches that had Pioneer Girls and Boys Brigade as their clubs curriculum because that is what Sally taught at our Cleveland church and she considered it an excellent tool.

One of those churches was downtown, quite different than the rural location of our house and lake. But we decided to visit it despite the eight-mile drive. ACAC was the fit we needed with sound teaching, warm friendship and a gradual connection with all five of our children. It had been hard to leave our beloved Pastor Couch, our families and our friends. Sally quickly immersed herself in Pioneer Girls and our God/Family link was rebuilt in Pittsburgh and became healthy and growing. What a gift from God. Only later did we realize how far and broadly Sally would mature in her Career path while I was maturing in mine at Alcoa and this God environment.

School was a very different matter. The elementary school was an immediate fit for Steve, Lynne and June. But Ken's middle school was a very harsh transition. The Fox Chapel school district is made up of several different communities with widely varying cultures. Some 7th graders tagged Ken as a Chappy (from wealthy Fox Chapel) and taunted him relentlessly and abusively. One of them knelt behind Ken in the hallway and a second boy pushed him onto the floor. Another time, a boy pushed him down the stairs. They stole his books and much more, all because he was a new kid and had moved into the wealthier part of the school district. Finally, after much prayer, enough was enough. Sally counseled him that it was time to fight back hard. He did, very aggressively, and the boys quit. Ken experienced the dark side of life. He thereafter developed close friendships with our neighborhood and church teens.

Our house became a counter-proposal to the experience Ken had in the 7th grade. When I recently asked our daughter Lynne to recall what our house had become within a few years of moving in, she answered that people would experience:

The house was open.

Just come in.

It's nice in here.

Nice because you're making me feel welcome.

You seem to like me.

And care about my needs.

My fear is passing.

You seem to like me the way I am.

You anticipated ways to help me.

I was surprised that you had

The bathing suit I needed,

The life preserver for me to wear,

Even the ice skates I can use.

And you helped me get the right size,

And weren't bothered when I tore the bathing suit.

You're orderly without being restrictive.

When I admitted my fears, you were kind.

You lessened my fears.

You were helpful and kind with my parents too.

They hated to admit that problem, but they trusted you.

I liked helping with cleanup. You made it fun.

It seemed like you were like Jesus.

That is the relational aspect Sally had built into the physical design she had worked out with our builder friend back in Cleveland a few years earlier.

Sunday afternoons at the lake in 1979

Soon we had our open house every Sunday from after the morning worship service until returning for the evening service. Typical attendance was about 30 but sometimes reached 45. Summer was water sports and winter was ice skating. In between was grass sports or indoor pool table, air hockey, table games and fellowship. We had three boats, 60 pairs of skates and about 40 bathing suits. We taught hundreds toward a thousand kids to water ski, which is a tedious learning/teaching process with about five tries per person.

Lunch and dinner were simple but tasty. Sally prepared them quickly on Saturday evening, timer cooked them while we were at church and managed the variability in numbers of people with rapid addition of spaghetti, macaroni and cheese, sandwiches, etc. such that she was always undaunted by the randomness of the number who came. Our five children and I operationalized all of the activities. We would rotate roles as boat drivers and in-water coaching as we taught water skiing because those two roles were tiresome.

One Sunday, a young man found our BB gun and shot out the windshield of five cars in our driveway. That led to some intense one-on-one counseling that turned out to be very effective for his growth. Another boy came to our house one day to bring back three matchbox cars he had stolen from our basement 15 years earlier. Our neighbors all around the lake were supportive of what we were doing. That acceptance carried forward to recent years when we host 400 summer day campers (35 per day for 12 days) with much action and noise. Praise God. Once again, they know and support the activity in the backyard. Little did we know at the time when Sally recovered from her cold day laying sewer pipes in Cleveland that God had intent for a lake and home. Our children were growing up as hosts and hostesses within God's kingdom.

12

Learning to Lead

During this season of open houses every Sunday, Steve was invited in 1974 by a neighbor family to travel to Vail, Colorado to ski. He had a great time and shared his experience with his siblings. So Sally helped the five kids pass out a notice throughout the neighborhood so they could earn money and all go to Vail. They got many jobs, did them well and deposited all earnings in a bank account they called "The Vail Ski Fund." I was the odd man out. I didn't know how to ski and this skiing activity conflicted with hockey time on our lake.

Well, an opportunity opened up: our friends sold their condo in Vail, which caused a setback for their ski trip plan. I seized the moment and counter proposed: "How would you like to go to England for a two-week period during which your mother and I will obey you?" Wow, did our kids ever like that idea – the power to pick the itinerary, destination, meals, etc.

They immediately diverted the Vail money to five airplane tickets to London. Sally and I covered the other costs for a camper, etc.

When they told their friends what they were doing, the Russells from Cleveland (Pat, Jim and three kids) asked if they

could join us. This posed a dilemma. All five were great friends to us, but Pat was strong willed and may find it difficult to obey her children as they chose the itinerary. We agreed to go together, travel in two motor homes and split up if Pat couldn't adapt. Our kids shared the good news about the experiment and recruited three more travelers; Ralph Garlick, (my classmate from Case); Brent Scott from the Vail ski family; and Bob Bliss, son of my Case friend Cy Bliss.

All 15 of us arrived in New York in 1976 for our flight to London but with only 14 passports. Janet Russell called her uncle in Cleveland, who put the passport on a flight to New York, thence to London and that assurance persuaded the airline to board Janet with us instead of holding her and her mother back for a day in New York.

The two vans used in the Europe adventure

Can you believe that we put 15 people in those two little campers? Well, we did. We had two little tents to ease sleeping if our overnight stop accommodated them. When necessary, all 15 slept inside the campers, with the two smallest children sleeping in the overcab baggage compartment. It was amazing to watch the 11 children lead. It only took one day for Pat to catch onto the power of this child experiment and to watch, rather than to decide. The only restriction for the children was to return the caravans to London 14 days later. There were no cell phones or communications so the front van "owned the day" and the rear van had to follow, no matter the route. Then they switched positions the next day.

They also shifted who was in which van, keeping Jim and Pat as drivers of one van and Sally and me as drivers of the other. Since active kids were making the decisions, stops to discover were frequent – mountains were meant to be climbed and water was meant to be experienced. Although the Brits would simply observe their Water Staircase, our leaders-in-training would climb into the water stairs and fountain pool.

When we traveled between Glasgow and Edinburg, the drive time in the vans was longer than ideal so I offered the kids one shilling per round trip for them to run up to the castle and back to the road. It worked great as a way to work off their excess energy and get loads of shillings from me. However, when they finished running, we were shy one person – Jim, our seven year old. We all fanned out to find him. On his very first trip, he had turned left and wandered into a shopping district instead of returning to the van to earn his shilling. We had set up a communication plan that anyone lost would call back to Mary Bliss in the United States and the people in the van would call Mary to find each other. We found Jim before that loop was necessary.

The venture into "Learning to Lead" was so successful that everyone wanted to repeat it the following year, but longer and on the continent. They all went back to work, saved their money and returned to London for a three-week trip. Once again, we arrived in New York with 15 people and 14 passports and had to get last minute help from the US Embassy to be able to board all 15 on the flight to London.

We rented the same type of vans, crossed the English Channel on a hovercraft and looped through France to Germany and onward.

Steve and Jim at the hovercraft

Our kid leaders became so adept that they repurposed the vans based on their preferences. Pat and Jim preferred a good meal and a secure campsite to end each day. However, the rowdies on the trip would rather have excitement and peanut butter sandwiches late into the evening. For example, as we approached Amsterdam in the Netherlands, some of our travelers moved into the Pat and Jim van and found a campground where they calmly ate, showered and slept. We had previously decided a reunion place for the next morning. Sally and I drove the rowdies into Amsterdam at night and stayed so long that there was no campground that would still be open. I drove into the night along roads with no pull offs (canals on both sides) until I found a road construction site that I parked in. At seven in the morning, some construction workers arrived and talked to me in a language I didn't understand. By their body language, I'm quite sure they were saying "get out, right now." I think I interpreted them correctly as they seemed less angry when I left.

All of us learned and grew by these two learn-by-doing experiences within our families. Don't be surprised that they used their newly improved leadership competence to persuade me to learn how to ski and then go with them on the Vail trip they delayed until I matured and saw the merit.

Article about the Europe trip in the Pittsburgh newspaper

13

Trial by Fire – August 1978

When I arrived at the lab at 7 AM on that day in August 1978, John Jacoby ran out to meet me. There had just been an explosion in the Fabricating Metallurgy Division lab that adjoined ours. A fire started in a furnace and four people from my division rushed over to help the three Fab Met people who were fighting the fire. Then the fire triggered an explosion and all seven were badly burned. Ambulances were arriving and departing. Four of the seven injured people were from my division as Manager of Ingot Casting Division. I had no knowledge about the furnace or what was in it so I told John, "I'll take the people side and the Division Manager of Fab Met can handle the on-site issues." Alcoa's doctor had already been alerted and he sent me the message: seven intense frontal burns, four were potentially fatal and all must go to the burn unit at West Penn Hospital about 14 miles away. I immediately raced there. The first departing ambulances went to the closest hospitals and were redirected to West Penn. I was therefore the first to arrive.

The men with burns began arriving and were hurriedly transferred into the burn unit. Then the first of the seven wives arrived. I only slightly knew Phyllis Baer but she rushed up to me and asked me if I was a born again Christian. When I said yes, she threw her arms around me and begged me to pray for Walt, her husband. She could not let go as she was overwhelmed with fear. I was her source of hope at that moment. Walt was one of the most seriously injured. I need not describe all seven wives or their children. I met them all, I wept with them and we prayed together. I stayed in the hospital forever, so it seemed. Several days later, the director of the lab came to the hospital and mandated that I go home. Period! So I went home, slept there for the first time since the fire and then went back to the hospital the next morning.

Severe burns like the ones sustained by these men remove the defense that our skin provides the body, thereby exposing the patient to all manners of potential system failures; heart, lungs, kidney, liver, etc. Every hour posed the possibility of death and the doctors of many specialties had to manage their part of each patient's trauma.

The Alcoa doctor was always aware of what was happening with all seven men. We soon made the decision that

I should not learn about an issue before the wife, a very kind and caring decision. Thereafter, I would be called whenever any of the seven incurred a problem, such that I (who lived closest to the hospital) could rush in, arrive before the wife, be caring and pray and then learn from her the news that the doctor had told her. That gave me the freedom to sleep at home, yet always be on site to help all of the wives every time the hospital called them.

Sadly, Hughie Fox died. We were all so very sad. I had become a close friend by then with his wife Dolly and their two children. I visited them for decades, always at Dolly's home. Trauma can shape very deep friendships. The other six all recovered, with Jack Zydonick taking the longest to recover. He was unconscious for more than a month. I bonded with his wife Carol and their two children. I was changed forever. Severe injury and death are so very hard to experience. God and love are so crucial at times such as these.

The year 1978 had other reminders of human frailty. Sally's mother Mary Ewing had multiple strokes and her father Bob Ewing broke his back as he picked her up from one of her falls. Mary died from her strokes one month after her brother Parlee Grose died and shortly before her sister Ruth Wasson died; three sibling deaths within six months. The explosion at Alcoa was within days of the death of the third of Sally's relatives.

Sally wrote the following in her Christmas letter:

Christmas 1978

It is said that we grow spiritually much more during our trials than our "mountain top" experiences, and this year has shown us much in His molding of our lives. We are so thankful for our five children... for their knowing the Lord as Savior, for their help at carrying on the home life so well in Keith's and Sally's repeated absences from the home for extended periods this year, and for their care, concern and prayers during the many trying moments we faced this year.

Sally's father died a few months later. Both of my parents died before we moved to Pittsburgh. There is a lonesome feeling to be without parents you have loved. But it is tempered by the assurance of heaven for Hughie Fox and our four parents.

There is a lesson about love in this portion of our life story. All of us need it and all of us can give it. Surely we must do that in marriage, with parents and with children. God designed us for that – it makes us whole. But there is another love – the one God calls "love thy neighbor." That love bathed all seven families of Alcoans at West Penn Hospital. Sadly, the majority of burn patients do not receive such love. The extreme trauma of a massive burn and the feeling of guilt (that it could have been prevented) can overwhelm the family members to such an extreme that they run away. It is difficult to handle the mood in the waiting room alongside the burn unit. Recovery rates are lower for patients fighting for their lives without love. I advise you – be a lover of the type God intended you to be. His way is the best way, the high side of life.

Within a year of the lab explosion, I was promoted to assistant director of the lab and shortly thereafter, the announcement from the consultants that ALCOA IS A MATURE BUSINESS, followed by their solution that was grossly insensitive to the people. God prepared me to be a spokesperson opposing such behavior; at work, at home, at church and in my neighborhood. By that time, I had a soft heart, but was not a pushover. Within another year, I was transferred out of the lab forever and into the mainstream of the business, Corporate Planning, as Manager Business Planning. I have written about this connectivity not to take you back to my business career, but to clarify how God's mentoring of me was for similar agendas in both domains: Family and Career. I remind you that the three threads of my book are interwoven: God, Family and Career.

His way is the best way, the high side of life.

These were the years of self-discovery for our children of carving out their own paths for life, even to the extent of rebellion. Our oldest son Ken graduated from high school and began college at Penn State and our youngest son was in 5th grade. Meanwhile, I was massively busy. God graciously provided other people to assist in these growth processes. For

Ken, He provided David Muhleisen, who was from our church and a classmate of Ken's at school. When the harassment of Ken increased during middle school, David (a strongly built teen) sought out the lead abuser, told him to stop and then punched him in the face so hard that his nose was bleeding. That ended the harassment and bonded Ken and David. Then God brought Tom and Jenny Keller to be youth pastors at our church and they were excellent one-on-one mentors. If a teen lifted weights at 7 AM, Tom would come to their house at 7 AM and lift weights too. If you practiced piano at 6 PM, Jenny would come to encourage you. They carried God's love to who you are and where you are. They became beloved friends and mentors of all of our children except Jim, who was too young. Several years later, the Kellers were in a too-small house in Florida, so Sally and our five children went to Florida and helped to build and to pay for a three-room addition. They built it in a week, then returned later for a second week to finish the interior.

Our children were friends of each other and did things together. They also developed strong friendships with our neighborhood kids and church kids, assisted by the every-Sunday open house. But they also worked together via their poster offering to do odd jobs that paid for Europe trips. Lawn mowing expanded to 38 lawns, which were large because Fox Chapel has minimum lot sizes of one, two or three acres. They mowed in pairs using a lawn tractor and regular lawn mower. Then, since Pittsburgh had lots of potholes, Ken launched his siblings and friends into a hubcap business in which they found hubcaps on the side of the road, straightened them and then sold several thousand salvaged hubcaps at about $5 to $10 per hubcap. Revenue was divided up at the end of each month by estimating the percentage of work in each of these three categories that was done by each person. They found a book showing the picture and retail price of every hubcap for every car. Our photo shows their trailer loaded and ready for a selling day at a local flea market. Their business strategy was high turnover at low prices because their upstream feed of hubcaps was fast and free.

Ken, friend Tim Anderson and Steve, 1979

Sports of many types were often and fun. Rarely did our kids play in a league or school sport. Instead, it was brothers, sisters, church friends, neighbors, older and younger playing at high speed but low injury. Such has continued to this day with hockey or ultimate Frisbee being played by our family nearly every Monday. These are carry forwards from the decade of

Sunday open houses. The major difference is that the 20 grandchildren and their 11 spouses are now outperforming their five moms and five dads with their speed and agility. The young 11 great-grandchildren are not yet five years old so they have an age-appropriate child game field alongside the Frisbee field. Our three threads God/Family/Career now continues into a 4th generation.

Frisbee in 2020, L to R: Noah, Paul, Addy, Addison and Lucy

14

Visioning

At the 25th anniversary of our marriage in 1982 and the beginning of the third decade of our parenting, we took our five children on a very special four-week vacation to Australia, New Zealand and Hawaii. Sally and I believed that it would be our last opportunity to have all seven of us together and wanted to celebrate how much we loved each other and loved God. I wrote about this in Chapter 10 because of its Career implications, but I have chosen to write again here to bring out its God/Family implications.

We planned the trip long before our anniversary and certainly before my just-before-departure promotion to Director, Technology of Planning, and before Lynne's just-before-departure broken foot caused by a tractor repair mishap with her brother Steve. We also planned it before the team of research planners learned just before departure that they had new jobs in corporate (rather than research) to do Technology Planning (which hadn't been defined yet), reporting to a boss who is now running away for a month. See you later! Why so? Because it was time to hear from God. Ken had graduated from college one month earlier. God - who is Ken to be? Will he marry, and if so, who? Steve had finished his first year of dental school because he passed the Pitt dental exam one year early and skipped his senior year of pre-dentistry. Soon he was to ask "What next?" Lynne was in her sophomore year at Wheaton College, majoring in nursing. June was to graduate from high school in a year and planned to go to Penn State. Jim was to soon enter high school. Sally wrote:

Christmas 1982

This year was characterized most vividly by our togetherness as a family.

Now to a focus point of the family togetherness we mentioned earlier: all 7 of us celebrated our 25th wedding anniversary with a 4-week vacation in August to Australia, New Zealand and Hawaii. We left for that trip as a close family, but returned even closer. How thankful we are for the common Christian faith we share! We are thankful for all these things which 1982 has offered: for the laughs (such as when Jim had a boxing match with a kangaroo and lost), for the special friends and relatives whom we love, for the testings (such as a terrible storm as we spent a wind-whipped night on a boat on Australia's Great Barrier Reef), for new experiences (such as the kids learning to SCUBA) and for old favorites (like ice skating on our lake on crisp winter days) ... and for everything God uses to help us to grow. We sincerely hope that Christ is the reason for your celebration of this beautiful season. May '83 bring you ever closer to Him.

Vision 1- Love All People

The first God lesson we learned was how much we displease God when we discriminate against a people group and how sweet it is when we choose to love them instead. Australia had been a penal colony within the British Empire, a place they sent criminals that they might otherwise have put in prison. These white people looked down on the dark-skinned natives they called aborigines, thinking of them as sub humans. They even took children away from their mothers to school them the British way as a way to "improve" them. God was preparing all seven of us for a strong lesson in how He loves all people.

While we were staying at the home of the Pinjarra plant manager (the man I had worked with in Pittsburgh Corporate Planning), he shared some experiences. An employee at the plant came to work one day with several tools. He said to his boss, "Several years ago, I stole these from our plant. But now I've become a Christian and God told me to return them. I know that you can and should fire me, but you will be firing me after I've become a much better worker than before I accepted Christ." His immediate boss didn't know how to handle it so the decision escalated all the way to the plant manager who decided to not fire the had-been thief.

As Sunday approached, we asked our host where we could go to church. He was not a churchgoer but recommended several nearby, though with the admonition not to go to a particular church because it was doing "bad things." We became curious, checked the church out further and then attended that church. It was a Christian and Missionary Alliance Church, the same denomination as our home church. It turned out to be "bad" because it was the church of the thief who had returned the tools and it had both white and aborigine members blended together as caring friends. On that Sunday, they were praying for a missionary couple and their children who had been trained in this church and were now moving to northwestern Australia to start a like-church in an all-aborigine sector. The missionaries were aborigines. The message from God to us was profound. God loves all people, for certain the ones that people choose to repress. The seven of us learned the lesson that the United States must repent for our sins upon Native Americans and African Americans. Like the thief from the Alcoa plant, God offers healing and reconciliation if we ask Him and obey.

Vision 2- God Protects

Our second God lesson emerged during an overnight stay on a sailboat anchored above the Great Barrier Reef off the east coast of Australia. We traveled north past the last big city of Brisbane to the area called Whitsunday Coast, 80% up the coast of Australia. The road became so deserted that road-killed animals were left in the road. Vehicles were equipped with large steel grills called roo bars so the animal would lose and the vehicle would win during a collision. Our family counted the dead kangaroos and quit when the count got to 70. There were also seven wild cattle and three horses.

Sally with the anchored sailboat in Australia

When we arrived at Whitsunday, we boarded a pontoon plane and flew to the Great Barrier Reef. A smaller boat met the plane and transferred us to the anchored sailboat. Such trips were normally a few hours long, but we were the last trip of the day and that trip overnighted in the sailboat. We anchored in the center (the hole) of a giant donut-shaped reef encircled by a part of the reef that is above water at low tide and slightly below water at high tide. At our location, the water depth was about 15 feet. We fished and scuba dived off of the small boat that had transferred us from the plane. These details are important because a storm was coming our way with high winds. A regular sailboat saw the storm coming and sailed into our donut so they would have some protection from heavy waves. They set their anchor, but as the waves intensified, the anchor would release and they would have to motor upwind and reset the anchor. Our anchor was massive and permanent so we stayed attached, but bounced around all night. The ongoing work of anchor slipping/anchor resetting was

223

exhausting the people in the other boat, so all but one of our crew left us and helped the other boat all night long to not crash on the reef. We had a night of fear, faith and sea sickness, trusting that our anchor would hold. When the winds weakened and the other boat was secured, all of the exhausted folks came into our boat and shared their story. Wow! How scary it was for them. How thankful they were that they were now safe. As they began to feel the relief of total safety, they shared their life stories of what it is like to be Australian, even singing boldly and loudly their favorite Australian song, "*Waltzing Matilda.*"

That is precisely what God provides for us in life – an anchor - if we will let Him. We were safe. How assuring.

As we reflected on their stories and the night, we saw a profound God message to us. All of them and we were frightened as the winds became even more intense and the waves slammed against our boats. But ours was anchored to a rock – giant and unmovable – such that we did not have to be frightened. That is precisely what God provides for us in life – an anchor - if we will let Him. We were safe. How assuring. All seven of us learned a lesson in trusting God.

Vision 3 - People are Amazing

The third God lesson was learned during in an intentional three-day layover in Hawaii that we scheduled for our trip home. We had a great time touring the island and enjoying the scenery. As usual, the water, snorkeling, surfboarding, etc. were the primary interests for our forever-active children. It was hard for Sally and me watching our children jump off a high rock that they found. But it was even harder watching Steve as he walked up to the edge and then dove headfirst from such a high rock. He executed the dive perfectly, was not injured and continued his agenda to scare me enough times that all of my hair would turn grey.

The God lesson on Hawaii occurred when we visited Pearl Harbor on Oahu Island. Sally and I knew about Pearl Harbor since we were five and six years old as the place that the Japanese invaded and drew our country into World War II. The majority of Americans had not wanted to go to war prior to the bombing and our country was actively negotiating a peace agreement with Japan when they launched a surprise attack on Pearl Harbor to destroy our Pacific Ocean ships. In a single day, the entire United States closed ranks with our president and joined into what we called the War Effort. The ship Arizona remains sunken in the bay, its nearly 1,000 sailors entombed inside forever.

When I stood on its deck with my family, I looked up and down the harbor. I could not fathom how the people who had been attacked and others who rushed to help had refloated, repaired and sent to battle virtually every other ship with seemingly impossible speed.

Next Gen, the 1989 Model

At this 30th year of our family, a whole new generation formed up and did it with gusto. Ken, our first child born in 1959, married Sheri Bealer and they welcomed baby Jessica in 1987. Not to be outdone, June married Scott Wakeley one week before Jessica (the editor of this book) was born. Then, within 12 months, Steve married Marla Browning and Lynne married Ron Bogolin. Jim was too young to join the beginning of this surge but joined it four years later when he married Kristen Wilt.

Have no doubt about it, this second generation Sally and I now overlap commissions the two of us to a brand-new title – grandparenting. The five new families all moved rapidly forward into their generation with five marriages, five houses, five dogs and (in God's timing) 20 children. Sally's parents had been overtaxed with our mob of five. I can't even imagine how they would have responded to these 30 and their five dogs. But I do know how Sally and I responded. We were thrilled, loved them all and prayed that God/Family/Career would carry forward and grow stronger. As I write, another 30 years has passed and we are thrilled with the 12 marriages of our grandchildren (so far) and the 11 great grandchildren (so far). But let's look back at 1989 to see how it began.

The seven of us had interconnected God, Family and Career for certain. They are a powerful threesome. We worshipped together, worked together, played together and grew up together. Friends were welcomed and joined in. All five of our children became Christians, as did many of their friends. We all believed in God's principles and used them to set our directions. They led us to high sides such that drugs and smoking were bypassed, and alcohol was minimal, despite what classmates did. When each of the five went to college, two chose Christian colleges and the other three forged relationships via Christian campus outreaches. Those three went to Penn State, and became leaders in the on-campus, student-led Alliance Christian Fellowship church. Two of the three found their marriage partner there. All five married Christian spouses. Three of the five husbands became pastors. Praise God for the formation of these five families that by now were beginning to form up their generation that would move Sally and me into the roles of grandparents. All 12 of us (our children, their spouses, Sally and me) are imperfect people, even though we strive to know and to obey God's life principles. Some problems grew large and one divorce has occurred. Yet those parents have cooperated with each other to raise their children well.

Meanwhile, on the Career side, Sally immersed herself in Godly nurturing of our family and God's assignment to 5th grade girls from church, clubs and camps. She loved them, mentored them, shared with them that they were precious to

God and shared the salvation message that she had not heard when she was their age. Most of them were brought to our lake, some with their leaders for overnights. Every Wednesday evening before clubs, Sally would pick up one of her club girls at her home so that Sally could meet the girl's parents. She then took the club girl to a restaurant of the girl's choosing and they would have one-on-one time to talk about life, God and salvation. When the number of club girls grew to 32, it took until the end of the school year to meet with all of them.

Meanwhile, amazing things were happening with me in my Career area. I was, at the core, the same person at work and at home. But, because Alcoa was a global business operating in nations with all forms of religion and atheism, I could not impose my Christian faith. But I could live out my Christian ethics, so I did. I was therefore kind, caring and (as you might expect) highly intentional in connecting business discoveries and direction to the universe principles while living the life principles. Technology Planning had taken the query "What is the Theoretical Limit (the operative principle)?" for their processes to every plant for seven years. By 1989, Paul O'Neill had been CEO for two years invigorating all Alcoans and challenging them to know and act on these findings. Corporate President Fred Fetteroff even joined leaders of companies and unions (normally adversarial) together for a morning-long Labor Management Prayer Breakfast. It was a huge success, filling the grand ballroom of the William Penn Hotel; repeated multiple years and it was unapologetically Christian.

Concurrently, Rock Dillaman became the new pastor of our Pittsburgh church, arriving with a call from God that our plateaued inner-city church was to grow to 1,000 people and that we would grow from two adult Sunday School classes to 10. What amazing insights into God's power and intent for a congregation of primarily grey-haired people. Young families were the major source of growth, not just joining the church but also moving into the Northside neighborhood of Pittsburgh to stave off the urban decay that was rampant. Pastor Rock made it a priority to know the name of every single person in the congregation, a commitment he was able to achieve until we surpassed 1,000.

Then, as a second leading from the Lord, He led the church into intentional, loving, and God-powered diversification. He began with biblical-based sermons about the wrongness of segregation, then biblical-based sermons that broadened the music of our worship. Whereupon, based upon God's principles, we confessed, repented and reconciled such that we diversified based upon love, not regulations. It was beautiful to see and to be a part of.

The Magnitude of the Book

At the very beginning of this book, we declared it to be *The Life Story of Keith and Sally Turnbull* and we promised to share it with "honesty and uncommon candor." Chapter by chapter, line by line, the pieces of our life story have been written as an outpouring of our hearts: so sincere that we have shed tears as we wrote. Again and again, each time we edited sensitive segments, we cried anew.

Where does that all take us? To the very essence of this book, the climactic and most important four words I have written. By the 30th year of family, we had completed our generation and our five children were launching their generation's version of the precious two words: Marriage and Family. And where had Sally and I progressed? Amazingly, to the four words:

LIFE STORY
HIGH SIDE

Awesome. Beyond our wildest imaginations. We were elated earlier when we used five of God's principles to attain Marriage – High Side. Then we used one of His principles to attain Love Thy Neighbor High Side. And so it goes, page by page: in Alcoa, with the fifth grade girls, with our lake, etc. We weren't wise enough to see where God's overall plan was headed, so He took us step by step:

As Cousins in depression/death/stroke

As teenagers Wandering in the Wilderness

As beneficiaries of Falling in Love in a single day

As husband and wife married to the high side

As parents using Bruce Clark's prophetic advice from God

As a research scientist mentored into a business leader

The list could go on and on. But, precious reader, see the SIMPLICITY of it all; God's list isn't six such items or 12 or 18. It is just one: the last line of Lynn Rogers' song in our wedding - "Thy Kingdom Come, Thy Will be Done on Earth as it is in Heaven." Lynn then stopped abruptly, purposefully discarding the next lines "Give us this day our daily bread" and many more lines. Why? Because he had reached the pinnacle point of his prayer for us: SALLY AND ME, TO TRAVEL GOD'S KINGDOM ROAD HERE ON EARTH FROM THIS MARRIAGE DAY FORWARD TO FOREVER. God heard him and so did we. One week after our wedding, we moved forward onto "God's Kingdom Road," with the principle Leave and Cleave, then a second principle, One Flesh, thereafter whichever principle next applied.

This beautiful convergence began to become clearly describable as our children were marrying and raising their families and became quite clear now that our grandchildren are marrying and becoming parents.

I could stop here. I should stop here! The Grand Conclusion of the book has just been written. Movies and books carry us to a happy or sad ending and then send us on our way. But I must override that protocol because Blaine Workman and my children entrusted me to write a book of beginnings, not an ending book. Heather Kimpel, my granddaughter, read a portion of the book and challenged me to write for her daughter, Micah who is now eleven months old at this writing, to read and to do as she grows up and contemplates marriage. My granddaughter Allison Turnbull offered the same insight. And Blaine believes this story about God should be an ongoing encouragement for people to seek God. Therefore, I have three epilogue messages written beyond my Grand Conclusion; one to summarize God's mentoring me via the Key Principles that shaped my life; second to describe perpetual love; and third to provide for you a detailed Case Study showing you the "How To Do It" when moving to the High Side.

Grandkids in 1995

The Turnbull family in 2011

15

God's Perpetual Mentoring

From the very beginning of the book, I have described the three interwoven threads: God, Family and Career. You should not be surprised that God mentored me concurrently with all of the growth I was experiencing in Career. As you read my steps, ask yourself the question - "Am I letting God mentor me?" If so, what steps have you taken so far?

I begin this forward advice to you and to our great-granddaughter Micah by emphasizing the importance of engaging BOTH types of God Principles.

Universe Principles	Life Principles
God designed the universe,	We are made in God's Image,
With God's operating principles.	As His beloved image bearers,
We gradually discover them	With intrinsic value.
And call them science.	We're to love God.
They are the orderliness of;	Then our spouse and neighbor.
Physics,	His Bible tells us how.
Chemistry and	He helps us to obey Him.
Biology.	Life is best when we do.
We can use them.	We should use them.

This table is so important that I have chosen to restate it in paragraph form and then present my message to you a third time showing you how they impacted my life. The Universe Principles were designed by God and are controlled by God. They persist whether we know them or not.

When we discover them, we name them, call them science and can benefit by knowing them. The Life Principles are also designed by God but are released via free will for us to operate. His intent is that we love Him and love each other. God gave them all to us in the Bible, where He wrote them, described them and implored us to use them.

Obedience leads us toward High Side. I have written the 10 key principles God used in my life such that they may help you to choose yours:

As a Child: Principle - SAVED BY GRACE
"By grace, you have been saved, through faith..." Eph. 2:8-9

While Growing Up: Principle – TRANSFORMED MIND
"Be transformed by the renewing of your mind..." Rom. 12:2

As a Husband: Principle – LEAVE AND CLEAVE
"Leave father and mother and cleave to your wife..." Gen. 2:24

As an Engineer: Principle – SOLVE PROBLEMS
By hypotheses – Problem/Cause/Solution/Action/Measure.

As a Scientist: Principles – UNIVERSE AND LIFE
"In the beginning, God created heaven and earth." Gen. 1:1

As a Father: Principle – NURTURE YOUR CHILD
"Train up a child in the way he should go..." Proverbs 22:6

As a Manager: Principle – LOVE GOD, YOUR NEIGHBOR
"Love the Lord your God ... Love your neighbor..." Matt. 22:37-38

As a Strategist: Principle – HOLY SPIRIT LED
"Prophesy...Dreams...Visions." Joel 2:28

As a Leader: Principle – TRUST AND OBEY
"...You have come to royal position for such a time as this."
Esther 4:14

As a Steward: Principle – USE GOD GIVEN TALENTS
"Well done, good and faithful servant..." Matthew 25:21.

Your life story will of course differ from mine and from Sally's. Use my list as a sample that guides you to your principles, the ones God intends for you. They are paths to the High Side of your life.

16

Perpetual Love – In Sickness and In Health

My second story is the next segment in the LIFE STORY HIGH SIDE of Sally and me. In 2003, I retired from Alcoa but Sally and I did not retire from traveling that Kingdom Road in the ways that God next intended for us. Sally and I now had time together – precious time – to travel in our motorhome from coast to coast in the United States and Canada. We, of course, saw God's beauty, but most importantly, we visited many of the 750 friends and family to whom we send Christmas cards every year. We shared elements of our Life Story to encourage them in their life story in ways that God directed. Sometimes we stayed several days helping a widow to solve her "to do list" for which she needed help. We equipped our motorhome with tools for most such tasks and purchased materials as needed. Often, what was most needed was love, encouragement and kind counseling as God directed.

Back home, we basked in the love of our family as it grew to the 55 we are now in 2020. We love our church family and greatly increased our time with them and doing volunteer work within the church's ministries. God expanded His agenda for our lake as we host baptisms, day visits by the 400 plus summer camp children (30 per day) from our church and Urban Impact Foundation, and more.

Then, at the halfway point (2012) of our retirement thus far, we picked up a traveling partner: MDS. We were in our motorhome in Florida with our dear friends Jim and Jackie Fudale when Sally became suddenly weak. We were sent back to Pittsburgh for further diagnosis and treatment. The finding: Sally has cancer, MDS: Myelo Dysplastic Syndrome. In layman's terms, her bone marrow is no longer making enough properly formed red blood cells to carry oxygen from her lungs to her body, thereby weakening her body.

The love that eluded us for three years, then was attained in one day, and consummated by marriage three years later is a forever love that was poised to be deepened even further. My high energy wife moved from a normal red blood cell count of 14-16 to a lower norm of 8-10. The only cure doctors have discovered thus far is a bone marrow transplant from a closely-matched donor such as a sibling. However, the transplant is so risky that it is only recommended for young patients, and even they have a 30% mortality rate from the procedure. However, there are life extenders and Sally's MDS was at a low level when initially diagnosed. Eight and a half years later, bi-weekly shots of Arenesp (a bone marrow stimulator) and regular transfusions of donor blood sustained Sally at this low level but she has gradually weakened.

At the lake in 2020

She thinks she is a burden to me, but she is wrong. It's true that she no longer pours concrete, climbs ladders or shovels snow. But this is like the problems of our honeymoon with overheated car/sunburn/mosquitos/engine troubles – mere nuisances! Our love is our love and God is our perpetual companion. We're delighted to be together. As we deepen our love and I do the household chores like laundry, Sally continues her lifelong ministry of sending personalized encouragement notes to whomsoever needs them every day, limited only by her physical strength that requires several naps per day. God made her that way, mentored her and assigned her to a career of loving children. What a privilege it is to be the man she loves.

Our children with their families, our church with our fellow believers and our friends with their kindness have supported us with love beyond measure. For Sally and me, our marriage covenant IS "love Sally, comfort her, honor and help her in sickness and in health ... as long as we both shall live." You bet! It took four years for me to get her to love me and three more before we could covenant that love via marriage. There's no other way but for us to deepen our love when cancer and age intrude. Furthermore, the forever dimension of our love means that we both are certain that death is merely the gateway to heaven, where we will spend eternity together with our Savior.

We trust that you'll share the faith we have in God so that we can share eternity with you, our precious reader, who has stayed with us as we have shared the life lesson of our

LIFE STORY
HIGH SIDE

17

Food Ministry – A Case Study

As a summary to draw together the learning lessons of my book, I've written an actual case study to show you how to apply your learnings to a situation closer to your life than the large Alcoa Corporation was. I pray this example will challenge you to consider how you can transform your work, ministry or home, using the Principles God gave us. You do not need to run a kitchen – the same transformation used for the Food Ministry can be applied in your workplace or wherever. I have chosen the transformation that we did with Food Ministry within our church to describe the broad change, but also the step-by-step smaller details.

When we were a smaller church, we had meals for events like weddings, funerals and special ministry celebrations.

People prepared an appropriate meal that they cooked at home or in the church kitchen. Food would be purchased, prepared, cooked and served. The number of people coming was almost always uncertain, so excess food was purchased. The ministries and food preparers believed that it would be very embarrassing to run out of food during a meal.

As the church grew larger, the frequency and size of meals grew. Then ongoing meals were added; every-weekday meals for the children in the six- or eight-week summer day camps, the every-Sunday breakfast and lunch for the multi-service church and the every-weekday lunches for the expanding weekday ministries. Meals were changing in size, frequency, type, duration, presentation and pervasiveness. We therefore upscaled it to become the Kitchen Ministry with a full-time leader, some staff and volunteers. It worked, but it was hard. After several years, the ministries like Adult, Student and Children were disappointed with the price and performance such that they primarily reverted to the do-your-own meals of the small church model. Furthermore, the Kitchen Ministry staff was tired by the overall process and saddened by the complaints. They also had overspent their budget by $44,000.

Reflection Question:
Have you experienced this stress at your work, ministry or home? Has tension emerged even when all of your coworkers desire to do good work?

Conventional Problem Solving

A commonly used way to handle such a situation could be to analyze the Kitchen Ministry to look for its problems and then devise and carry out a solution for each. Stay with me as I share the conventional ways that a situation like this might have been addressed. It quickly became obvious that:

The kitchen had Problems:

1. Ministries won't give us accurate headcounts – says the scheduler.
2. They complain that our prices are too high – says the menu writer.
3. Ministries "do food" themselves 80% of the time - says the kitchen head.
4. We're $44,000 over budget – says the church treasurer.
5. We're worn out and angry with the ministries and each other – say the food workers.

All five are true and are actual problems. Regular problem solving might be to immediately devise a solution for each of the five, as follows:

1. Ministries won't give us accurate headcounts.

    a. *So, get right numbers by having eaters preregister.*

2. They complain that our prices are too high.

    a. *So, use cheaper foods and smaller quantities.*

3. They "do food" themselves 80% of the time.

    a. *So, mandate that they cannot "do food" themselves.*

4. We're $44,000 over budget.

    a. *So, we will save $22,000 with these changes.*

5. We're worn out and angry with the ministries and each other.

    a. *So, impose punishments for arguing and fighting.*

I admit that these solutions are a bit crass. I did that to catch your attention. But, did you notice? We didn't draw GOD into the problems via His PRINCIPLES. Nor did we seek and find the CAUSE. Read the five again to see how easy it is to skip God and also to rush to a SOLUTION for a problem without first determining CAUSE. Then, did you notice also how grossly out of sync solutions 1, 2, 3 and 5 were with respect to God's loving set of Life Principles? Clearly, it is time to correct our hurriedness of skipping God's Principles and going Problem/Solution instead of Problem / Cause / Solution / Action / Measure.

Reflection Questions

How do you solve problems? Did the initial solutions above seem reasonable to you? Did you initially miss the God component? And the CAUSE?

The Problem
As Seen Using God's Principles

So let's start over, addressing these same five problems, but this time bringing in God, His intent and His Principles as we look for the CAUSES we previously ignored.

Problem #1 – "Ministries won't give us accurate headcounts."

- The search for CAUSE often requires five Whys:
    - Why 1 – Ministries don't include headcount when they order a meal.
    - Why 2 – People don't tell ministries if they're coming.
    - Why 3 – People come to WORSHIP GOD; food is incidental.
    - Why 4 – God's principle is "ALL WHO WILL COME," an open door.
    - Why 5 – Wow! Imposing "headcount" impairs GOD'S INTENT.

At this point, we have our CAUSE for Problem 1. Let's move forward to Problem 2 because they're related.

Problem #2 – "They complain that our prices are too high."
- The search for CAUSE (5 Whys again)
    - Why 1 – Our price is high because our cost is high.
    - Why 2 – We prepare meals without knowing headcount.
    - Why 3 – We oversupply because undersupply is bad.
    - Why 4 – The price to those who eat bears the cost of the excess.
    - Why 5 – OVERSUPPLY due to no headcount IMPAIRS GOD'S MINISTRY.

I'll skip the details, trusting that you can easily see that

Problems 3, 4 and 5 are simply the collateral damage derived from Problems 1 and 2. Before moving on, read the initial Problem/Solution list from 1 to 5 again, this time seeing how the Five Solutions listed would have impaired the ministries and God's outreach that He intends through food. Sometimes solving problems one by one works well, but for this situation, they behave like the carnival game called whack-a-mole. Every time you "hammer down a mole" – in this case it is "solve a problem" – a new one pops up to replace it.

<u>Reflection Questions:</u>

Is your gut reaction to do "whack a mole" problem solving? Is it challenging to do a new way to problem solve?

The Cause
As Detected to Root Cause

Clearly, our problem is large and is showing up as if Problem 1 "can't get accurate headcounts" is the dominant cause, but is it the <u>root</u> cause? Not really. It is at the center of the fray but isn't the root cause. Instead, the analysis of these five problems revealed that the food dilemma is a by-product of God's incredible blessing that moved ACAC from small church to large church, which in turn overstressed our small church food design. The previous standalone meals were so infrequent that they could easily be handled by: a funeral meal, then a gap, a wedding meal, then a gap, a ministry celebration meal, then a gap – days apart. These were suitably handled by a food design called BATCH --- BATCH. Batch is a standalone event, in this case a meal, that has its own design and execution, quite independent of any prior or subsequent event. But now, our batches are bigger and closer together, even to the point of overlapping. We've also overlaid summer camp meals and weekday café meals, both of which are extended meals (hours long), not normal BATCH meals.

The five problems, now seen as a linked set, clearly exposed the failure of BATCH---BATCH to service the wide array of ministries God intended for ACAC: the root cause is therefore BATCH. Our meals became randomized like the bumper cars at a carnival that frequently run into each other.

The Solution: Continuous Flow Can Solve Root Cause

This discovery that our church growth had outgrown BATCH---BATCH is extremely important. Why? Because the first five problems were process problems, whereas BATCH---BATCH is a system problem! The people within each of the five problems were victims trapped within an incapable system. Fortunately, there was an alternative system called CONTINUOUS FLOW. It could be adapted to our Food Ministry and solve our BATCH---BATCH system problem and all five of our process problems. How very fortunate. I have chosen this Case Study purposely so that you can learn how to apply my book to both the process and system aspects of your life story.

CONTINUOUS FLOW was a great way to improve our Food Ministry, but changes of this magnitude scare most people because of the perceived impact the new system may have upon their jobs and lives. Often those fears are warranted because the leaders of change pay too little attention to God's purpose and His Life Principles. Recall how severe and lasting the fears were when Alcoa's system change was announced as "MATURE BUSINESS" and essentially ignored the people concerns. For this transition, our very first step was to seek and discern God's purpose. It was:

God's Chosen People
Serving God's Food
to God's Family

The seven of us were His chosen team and each of us would have a role in designing and deploying Continuous Flow while concurrently operating BATCH---BATCH such that no meals would be compromised. Every week, we had a one-hour training session to lessen people's fears and to add the skills required for Continuous Flow.

To equip you for both process and system changes in your life story, I've chosen to write the Food Ministry system transition first, followed by the detailed training sessions.

CONTINUOUS FLOW is a People-Designed Principle with many uses including some restaurants. Flow is attained by linking several processes that people do to satisfy customer needs. Its principles are: sequentially-linked processes, flowing smoothly in the same direction, with easy connections, adaptable to customer need, with built-in problem solving. The linked processes for the food were acquire / prepare / cook / serve. It could be adapted to our church and attached to God Principles as a replacement for BATCH---BATCH. Our adaptation of it would take all of the meal types (funeral, wedding, summer camp, etc.) that I've listed and link them together as if they were a continuous stream of meals varying in type, time and quantity based upon customer need and want. This design worked for us because we could use basic food types like chicken that can be deployed into more than 20 tastes and presentations to accommodate the preference in each meal. Ministries would enter their meal choices to our Event U information system 14 days in advance and list their meal preference and the approximate number of eaters. Since this sounds radical, I will describe it a second time.

Let's consider it to be a single meal 14 days long. But it is a peculiar single meal in that it adapts along the way to accommodate the actual number of people who show up during each time interval, and serves them the food type most appropriate for their meal whenever it is throughout the 14 days. For example, Joe Grondziowski can use chicken over the course of 14 days to provide café meals, then a student ministry event for about 50 people, etc. with more than 20 appropriate taste changes, with chicken being used for chicken parmesan to chicken salad and more. As chefs, Richard Minter and Joe can also design food choices like salads and desserts that can flow from one meal to the next meal.

This is a huge improvement for; God's ministries, the food people, those who eat, the budget guardians and all future users of the system. The budget over-cost that had been caused by oversupply, which had been caused by no headcount, can be reduced from 30-50% down to the 5% that is attainable with continuous flow.

At this stage, we are in great shape. We have sharpened our PROBLEM definition, found its ROOT CAUSE and have an excellent SOLUTION. Furthermore, the solution supports God's design intent to "minister to all who come" by now seamlessly "feeding all who come." All that is left now to solve the Food Ministry problem are the ACTIONS and MEASURES, the last two steps in God's Principles for Problem Solving.

Reflection Questions:

What is BATCH---BATCH? Can you see system designs in your home or at your work? Do you see systems that are impaired and ministry needing redesign? Parenting a 16-year-old requires a different system than one for a three-year-old.

The Actions
Changeover Done God's Way

As we launch into the ACTION step, it is important to recognize that changeover is a very large step for which we need God's direction, protection and empowerment. I will remind you again how badly this went when Alcoa changed its system from MATURE BUSINESS to DIVERSIFY. There was no apparent attention to the 37,000 people side during changeover or their subsequent post changeover roles. Fear and demotivation were the consequence. God's most precious resource – People – were not considered or valued. Therefore, we must do the work that the CONTINUOUS FLOW SOLUTION requires and we must do it in conformance to God's Principles. Concurrently, we must temporarily operate the BATCH---BATCH with its ongoing meals during the changeover period. Thereafter, we must effectively operate the new CONTINUOUS FLOW Food Ministry. See again how important it was that God led us to His intent:

God's Chosen People
Serving God's Food
To God's Family.

What a blessing it is to have such assurance and guidance. Our mantra, the purpose and the methods we were to use were to be in the wisdom of God and the power of God. Our roles were to trust, discern and obey.

Change is not easy, but God can and did shepherd us through it. The Chosen People were Carolyn Hager, Sonya Green, Rico Ed, Richard Minter, Joe Grondziowski, Ken Turnbull and the many volunteers who gifted their time to this important ministry of God. Actions had to be crafted "on the fly" because ministries were still ongoing and food was required every day throughout our buildings. I joined the Chosen People as their consultant. All of us needed to frequently return to those nine words of God to guide all of us through the changes He intended. Humility in leaders of change is important.

Our roles were to trust, discern and obey.

Some of the changes were straightforward and easy; others large, even frightening. We looked first at the five original problems, this time engaging God's Principles, the Cause diagnosis and the emerging impact of CONTINUOUS FLOW.

1. We had to submit to the fact that headcounts must always be subordinated to God's open door: "all who will come." This acknowledgement of God's need had clearly exposed its CAUSE, which CONTINUOUS FLOW solves.

2. We had to stop "pricing" our food and switch to "costing." The marking up of cost to price had hidden the many CAUSES underlying our food processes and were painful for the ministry leaders requesting food.

3. When Food Ministry (its new name) solved 1 and 2 by feeding all comers and serving them at cost (number of eaters X purchase cost of food = the charge to ministries), it totally eliminated the incentive of

problem number 3 for ministries to "do food" themselves. They did not need a "mandate." The new design was conspicuously superior, so they willingly used it.

4. The burden then moved to the budget. Will the causes now starkly exposed in 1, 2 and BATCH double the overbudget to $88,000 or trim it to zero? The $88,000 was an estimate of the possible risk from the price-to-cost change and was frightening, whereas the zero was the possible advantage of reducing overspend. But what does God intend? And how will these CHOSEN PEOPLE discover God's ways and will they have the strength to carry them out? The answer became yes, "they will know" and yes, "they will do" and the savings from overspend reduced the budget problem to zero.

5. Problem number 5 transitioned out of its worn out and angry trauma and into the excitement of changing over "on the fly." The food people did it and they pleased God with their obedience, which has now made them so strong that they could serve children 1,000 meals per day during COVID-19 in 2020.

Many other such improvements were made as we transitioned Food Ministry into CONTINUOUS FLOW. Linked meals were devised by Richard and Joe. Others did the food and its appropriate prepping, cooking and serving. By knowing WHAT was coming in the next 14 days, they neutralized the impact of HOW MUCH any particular meal in the 14 days would consume. They could see 14 days of forward food needs, buy weekly for the first 10 days, store this food frozen, refrigerated or at room temperature and then manage surges by using the 3-day buffer that was provided by the early buy of food that was needed for days 8, 9 and 10. Food types became important. For example, they could purchase and inventory a broad selection of basic food types like chicken from which they could provide a wide range of different tastes and presentation as preferred by each ministry.

Mentoring was necessary, frequent, intentional and caring: Carolyn et al mentoring Ken and me in food and Ken and I mentoring the five through the fears and uncertainties of changing over from BATCH designs to FLOW designs. The solution reduced leftovers (called shrinkage) from 35% to 5% so that the per person cost per meal went down and ministries were only billed for the actual meals eaten. Ministries could focus more on their God-given agendas and turn over virtually all meals to the Food Ministry. The budget balanced. Kind, caring teamwork replaced worn-out and sometimes angry ministry and food people.

The change from BATCH---BATCH to CONTINUOUS FLOW with linked meals 14 days long was a huge change for everyone. Our mantra of God's Chosen People, Serving God's Food, to God's Family was the calming, inspiring source for direction and healing. I included mentoring details in the Appendix so you can use the lessons in whatever way God is leading you in your Life Story so you can see the content and kindness required for the changeover and subsequent operation. Both derive from God's Principles. You can use this chapter and the Appendix as a model to transform your job, ministry or family.

At the very onset of changeover, we addressed the people aspects of changing the system from BATCH---BATCH to CONTINUOUS FLOW. These entailed Customer, Tasks and Teamwork; so in three one-hour sessions, we taught how these three enhanced the ways people work together. Then, we taught Flow and how we could make it continuous. That led to Inventory and Acquisition, the smooth weekly sourcing for each 14-day set of meals. These five are the lessons in PRINCIPLES and MENTORING from Chapter 7 of this book. Thereafter, we added the PROBLEM SOLVING so that the Continuous Flow can be sustained whenever problems occur. With the system and behavioral training thus completed, Richard and Joe used their chef skills to populate it with excellent menus fulfilling God's intent for "all who will come" to be ministered to by: God's Chosen People, Serving God's Food, To God's Family.

Appendix

I have included the actual Training Lessons that we used to manage the Changeover Process for the huge change from BATCH---BATCH to CONTINUOUS FLOW. This is the third time in the book that the mentoring progression is 10 steps long. I wrote 1 to 7, then Joe Grondziowski wrote 8 and 9, then I concluded by writing the 10th. As you read the 10, notice how they connect step by step into the competencies and the processes to convert both the people and their infrastructure into CONTINUOUS FLOW. You can use changeover lessons such as these when you do changeover in your work or ministry or family.

1. Customer

A BAD EXPERIENCE AS A CUSTOMER:	A GREAT EXPERIENCE AS A CUSTOMER:
• Have you ever had one? • What made it bad? • How did you feel? • Is it still fresh in your memory: o When? Where? Who? o What organization? • By contrast, do you recall: o Any other event that month? o Any other organization that month? • Does the disrespectful person remember you? Moral: Customers Remember Bad Treatment	• Have you had one? • What made it great? • How did you feel? • Is it still fresh in your memory: o When? o Where? o Who? o What organization? Moral: Customers Remember Great Treatment

WHO IS YOUR CUSTOMER?	DO YOU MEET CUSTOMER NEEDS?
• Do you have one here? • Who? • Anyone else? • When a task is assigned: 　o Do you listen to the task? 　o Do you do the task? 　o Then get another task? 　o Without thinking about the customer? Moral: Your Customers ARE: • GOD • His family & • The person to your right.	• Do you know their needs? • Are they different for: 　o God? 　o His family? 　o The person to your right? • For God, it is ministry: 　o He is using His meal to minister, 　o To your customers and you. • For His Family: 　o They are eating, 　o Fellowshipping, 　o And experiencing God. • For the person to your right: 　o God partners you to serve 　o And to experience God's presence. Moral – God is ministering through you.

<u>Customer Summary</u>

Serving "does tasks,"
Tasks have customers.
Tasks usually marginalize customers,
But they must not.
So ask:
who is my customer(s)?
what is/are their needs?
How can I do my task to meet their needs?
Can I be pleasant, engaging and smiling such that -

Moral – God ministers to you and to them.

2. Tasks

THE ASSIGNMENT	THE SETTING

To you – From the assigner.
The task - The assignment.
The customer
Your understanding,
Your knowledge,
Your skill.
Any clarification?
The assigner's attitude,
Your attitude,
The customer's attitude.
	• For this desired change:
	  o What do you start with?
	  o What do you change it to?
	• Where do you do it?
	• What tools do you need:
	  o Are they here?
	  o If not, can you get them?
	  o If you can't get, then what?
	• What materials do you need:
	  o Are they here?
	  o If not, can you get them?
	  o If you can't get, then what?
	• Do you interact with others?

THE PROCESSES	THE WORK

• What processes will you use?
   o Must you set up first?
   o Then, how many
      processes?
   o In what sequence?
   o With what supplies?
   o What tools?
• Can you do these processes?
   o Well?
   o Or just ok?
   o Or you can't yet do
      them?
• Will you ask for help?
• Are they the right processes:
   o Are you now doing
      them right?
	Work requires work!
	Is it your intent to do it?
	• To do it safely,
	• To do it well,
	• To meet the needs:
	   o Of the assigner,
	   o Of the customer.
	• Doing each process well.
	• Validating your output:
	   o Right type and quality,
	   o Right quantity,
	   o Right time,
	   o To right person.
	• With right attitude.

THE ATTITUDE	WORK WELL DONE
God's Chosen People: God's Food: God's Family. Do you consider yourself chosen? • You are. • God is shaping you via work, • Toward His plan for you. Do you believe it's His food? • It is. • You are stewarding it for Him. Do you believe you're serving God's family? • You are. • Food is His ministry, • To His family, His community.	Matthew 25:21 "Well done, good and faithful servant! You have been faithful with a few things; I will put you in charge of many things. Come and share your master's happiness!"

Tasks Summary

The Assignment

The Setting

The Processes

The Work

The Attitude

Work Done Well

3. Teamwork

TEAMWORK	DEFINITION

Have you experienced it?
• Each of you can think of an instance.
• What made that to be teamwork?
• Have you experienced the opposite?
  o No teamwork
  o What made that happen?
• Do you think teamwork is the norm?
  o People do it all the time?
• Or is it the exception?
  o People usually don't?
	Let's agree on a definition.
	• Starting with "team":
	  o People on a bus are just people,
	  o But sometimes they team,
	  o What does it mean to team?
	• Let's now consider work.
	  o People don't always work,
	  o But sometimes they work,
	  o What does it mean to work?
	• Now put them together
	  o Teamwork is:
	  o Doing work as a team and
	  o Doing teaming as you work.

GOD'S DESIGN AND CALLING	POSSIBLE AND NOW NECESSARY

• God designed us for teamwork.
  o We're to work,
  o To work well,
  o To be helpmates.
• Not to be
  o Lazy,
  o Sloppy workers, or
  o In isolation.
• So teamwork is a high calling.
  o As God's chosen people,
  o Serving God's food,
  o To God's family, via
  o Teamwork.
	• Teamwork is made possible in Food Ministry because:
	  o Everyone sees customer needs,
	  o Work is connected – prep/cook/serve,
	  o Tasks are linked
	  o Flow is continuous.
	• Teamwork is necessary in Food Ministry because:
	  o Batches are now removed,
	  o The team makes as customers arrive,
	  o Continuous flow requires teamwork,
	  o Tasks are interdependent,
	  o Yet rates change,
	  o Isolation would fail.
	• Teamwork is both possible and necessary.

LIVING TEAMWORK	THE BETTER WAY
So team members:	• Teamwork pleases God
• Do not isolate,	and is God's better way
o Do not work at cross	to work:
purposes.	o It's respectful,
• Instead they work:	o Builds us up,
o As a team,	o Gives meaning to
o Serving God and	work,
people,	o Strengthens us and
o Intentionally joined	o Grows us,
together in work,	o As we obey and serve
o Doing tasks well,	God.
o Communicating	
clearly,	
o Meeting their	
obligations,	
o Gaining satisfaction	
from work,	
o And their fellow	
workers,	
o And their satisfied	
customers.	

Teamwork Summary

Teamwork is an Experience.

Connecting Team and Work.

It is God's Design and Calling,

That is Possible and Now Necessary.

Team Members are Living Teamwork.

It's the Better Way.

4. Flow

FLOW	DISCOVERING FLOW

• A special word
• So far, you have learned:
  o Customers
  o Tasks and
  o Teamwork
• You will now ADD:
  flow.
  o Flow is a special
    word:
  o A very, very
  o Special word!
	What might flow be:
	What have you done today?
	• Your homework
	  assignment?
	• Things you've been asked
	  to do?
	• A menu?
	• A prioritized list?
	None of the above are flow,
	no matter how useful.

FLOW FLOWS	**DISCONTINUOUS FLOW**

Flow is:
• The linked series,
• Of processes,
• People do,
• To satisfy,
• Customer needs.
 	
Thereby:
Flow flows.
Sometimes discontinuously
and sometimes
continuously.
	• Flow usually is
	  discontinuous,
	• Stop and start, with
	  queues, and waste.
	• Dissatisfied customers,
	• Frustrated suppliers.
	
	• Discontinuous flow seems
	  necessary
	• But is not necessary.
	
	• Its fluctuation frustrates.

CONTINUOUS FLOW:	CONTINUOUS FLOW REQUIRES:

• Begins with the customer:
  o What is the need,
  o Learn it clearly.
• Then the processes:
  o Which are needed,
  o To do what,
  o In what sequence.
• And the people:
  o Who do the processes (their tasks),
  o Such that they meet customer's needs.
	• Knowing customer need,
	• Right processes,
	• People:
	  o Who serve customers
	  o Who do tasks well
	  o Who do teamwork
	• Tools (and machines),
	• Material,
	• Information,
	• Rhythm and
	• Problem solving.

Flow Summary

Flow is a special word.
Not just scheduling and doing.
Flow Flows: processes/people/customer
Marginalized if Discontinuous
But very effective if Continuous
Read on: Food is becoming Continuous.

5. Inventory and Acquisition

Is more than accounting.
It is an element within flow.

INVENTORY IN DISCONTINUOUS FLOW:	INVENTORY IN CONTINUOUS FLOW
• Separates processes, • Which then run at different rates. • With excess or stock out. • Gets stale and damaged. • Accrues unneeded items. • Such bulking up of inventory prevents replenishment from being clear, so • Such inventory is "Dead." • "Dead" inventory doesn't "talk."	• Connects processes • Which then run at same rates. • No excess or stock out. • Not stale or damaged. • No unneeded items. • No bulking up of inventory enables replenishment to be clear, so • Such inventory is "Live." • "Responds to requests" and "asks to be replenished."

LIVE INVENTORY "TALKS"	ACQUISITION:

• Because it's integrated with flow.
• It enables flow to match menus
• Even when flow surges or slows.
• Because it "buffers" the meals,
• Reveals right/wrong, and
• Reveals ahead/behind.
• Each store lane (food type) "talks"
• Talking that:
  o Confirms calmness,
  o Triggers to replenish.
  o By the equation: Rate of use X time to replenish + case pack size.
	• Is calm,
	• Caused by flow,
	• And triggered by "live" inventory.
	• In each store type whether
	  o Frozen
	  o Refrigerated or
	  o Dry.
	• When any lane (type) reaches its "trigger"
	  o Based on menus,
	  o The surge and slowdowns menus cause,
	  o Linked directly to food type.

Inventory and Acquisition Summary

Food ministry can minister
Serving God and His family,
As servers serve,
In a calm flow of food,
Drawn from secure inventory:
Sufficient and fresh.
In stores of food that "talk":
Right/wrong
Ahead/behind and then
Trigger replenishment
Via acquisition linked to
Triggers and
Menus.

6. Problem Solving

ALL OF US HAVE EXPERIENCED PROBLEMS AND LEARNED:		
	Yes	No
Problems are bad		
Look first for "who"		
Then fix the problem		
And punish the person		
Based on problem severity		
So the person doesn't repeat		
Therefore		
People conceal problems		
So they're not caught		
And don't "rat on friends"		

No wonder problems are bad!

LET'S START OVER BY CHANGING KEY WORDS:	WHICH REDEFINES PROBLEM SOLVING
• Bad to Good • Who to What • Fix to Cause/Solve • Punish to Engage • Severity to Root Cause • Person to Problems Therefore • Conceal to Reveal • Caught to Engaged • Don't rat to Team With	• Problems are good • Look first for what • Cause/solve problems • The person engages • Based on Root Cause • So problems don't repeat Therefore • People reveal problems • So they're engaged • And team to grow People work in the right environment to detect and solve problems.

RIGHT STRATEGY	BUILD THE RIGHT ENVIRONMENT:

Problems that can haunt food servers are prevented from getting started via:
• Vision
  o God's Chosen People
  o Serving God's Food
  o To God's Family
• Design
  o These 9 Design Steps
• Servers
  o God's teamworkers
  o Obeying God.
Thereby enabling mentoring via problem solving.
	So that workers can know and meet customer needs
	• Right tasks
	• With food safety
	• Linked to customer needs
	• Via menus
	• Which flow (continuously)
	• From acquisitions and inventory
	• With near zero shrink
	• Caused by connected menus
	• And teamwork
	Within CONTINUOUS FLOW.

GROWTH	GOD'S METHOD

God grows His people via Problem Solving:
 	
• In the fertile soil
• Where work works
• And flow flows
• And teamwork flourishes
• Such that customers are delighted.
 	
Punitive approaches to problems are alien, replaced by constructive mentoring.
• Solve every problem close in:
  o Time
  o Place
  o Person
  o To Its occurrence
• People detect and solve problems
• So that they mentor each other
• As they solve problems as they occur.
	Problem Solving is vested by God:
	• Every child uses HIS method
	• People call it the Scientific Method
	• Scientists didn't invent it
	• They discovered God's method
	• And gave it the fancy name of
	
	HYPOTHESIS (which has 5 steps)
	  1. Problem
	  2. Cause
	  3. Solution
	  4. Action
	  5. Measure
	
	Mentored people in fertile soil:
	• Aren't repressed or punished
	• They use God's method to solve problems
	• As they serve God and His family.

7. Overall Design for Continuous Flow

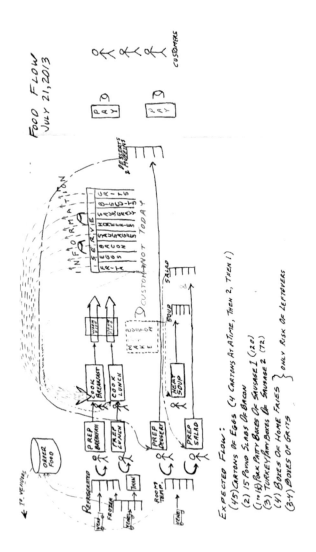

8. Menu Overview

There are seven steps to Menus and Meals:
- A. Inventory
- B. This Week's Meals and Flow of Food
- C. Customer Tastes
- D. Ordering Process
- E. Receiving
- F. Production
- G. Serve

A. INVENTORY (Counting, On-hand Food)

Richard inventories all food and supply products in the food pantry areas – ready for use foods includes

Frozen

Fresh

Canned

Paper

This is usually done on Tuesdays in the morning.
Richard does this process because he can multitask other processes as he inventories:
- Check dates of product.
- Check rotation (First In, First Out).
- Checks leftovers.
- Checks temperatures.
- Checks cleanliness.
- Checks organization of products.

B. THIS WEEK'S MEALS

We plan:
- Any catering meals Wednesday through following Thursday, 9 days ahead
- This Sunday's breakfast and lunch and how they can integrate into flowable meals.
- We monitor "shrink" – very powerful word – or waste at every meal

C. CUSTOMER TASTES

- Our catering menus have been created to use "standard" food items
  - Standard = Chicken, 20 different ways,
  - Potatoes, 10 different ways
  - Veggies, 6 different ways, etc.
- Richard has menu items that are proven sellers. The menus also have items that are season specific.
- Menus can change:
  - Customer wants and desires
  - Flow of catered events
  - Holidays
    - Any donated food
    - Excessive leftovers

D. ORDER PROCESS

- Richard will order from Sysco, Sam's, Costco, Restaurant Depot.
- Richard replenishes "pantry" items to a par level that will accommodate many meals and some unexpected meals.
  - o Par level = how much is needed to serve meals until the next order arrives.

E. RECEIVING

- Items are received, inspected, dated and organized on shelves and coolers/freezers.

F. PRODUCTION

- Lists are made for each food type that is being served.
  - o What we need for a particular menu
  - o What we have on hand
  - o What we have to produce

We do this for the entire menu.

- Multiple sections are then divided out into areas for workers to prepare.

G. SERVING

Products are assembled into proper serving pans and are hot/cold held or immediately consumed on the serving line, refrigerators, or deli case.

9. Connected Menus

There are five steps to Connected Menus:
- **H.** Inventory
- **I.** The 14-Day Outlook
- **J.** The Plan
- **K.** The Menus
- **L.** Execution – The Flow

H. INVENTORY

As stated in the previous menu section, we inventory all of our food products, ready-to-eat, canned, frozen and dry goods. Our "pantry" or "store" has levels of food that need to be available for a period of 10 days "cycle." This cycle time is figured out by:

- Ongoing food needs (standard items = par level)
- The number of days between inventory and when the food arrives in the pantry.

Inventory on Tuesday am
T+W+R+F+S+S+M+T (inv)+W+R (food arrives) = 10 days
- Special orders – don't upset us!
- Increased menus = catering

The orders are placed electronically.
- o Sysco Food Service, Sam's Club, Costco, Restaurant Depot, Giant Eagle for emergency supplies and very small needs, ie small bunch parsley

I. THE 14-DAY OUTLOOK

- Event-U – our interministry ordering process
  - Ministries order their food needs through an event menu online. These "events" are scheduled by Tuesday of every week by 4 pm. Ministries are encouraged to order as far ahead of time as possible.
- UP Café is open for business every week from Tuesday thru Friday, 11:30 am to 2 pm
  - o Highlighted items – daily lunch specials, stocked self-serve coolers, salad bar each day
- The "Sunday Meals" – average of 330 meals per day
  - o Meals created for church family to enjoy on Sunday between 7:30am – 2 pm

J. THE PLAN

- Food Ministry compiles information about Event U events (ministries), Sunday meals, UP Café weekly line-up
- Food is ordered from appropriate purveyors.
- Works lists are made.
- People are assembled (staff and volunteers).
- Menus are executed.

K. THE MENUS

- Food Ministry has multiple menus that are chosen by a ministry, or Sunday Meal is prepared out of "Core" ingredients.
  - o One 6-oz chicken could be: Stuffed chicken, BBQ chicken, Cajun chicken, Crispy chicken, etc.

L. EXECUTION – FLOW OF MENUS

Wednesday
- Event U menu – Student Ministry – Picnic
  - Grilled chicken, hamburgers, potato salad, fruit
- UP Café
  - Turkey sandwich special, hot dog/fries, salad bar

Thursday
- Event U menu – Children's Ministry Church in the Park
  - Hamburgers, pasta salad, fruit, cookies
- Event U menu – Women's Bible Study kickoff meal
  - Crispy chicken, French fries, vegetable, fruit
- UP Café
  - Hamburgers, hot dogs, chili, salad bar

Friday
- Event U menu – Care Connections kickoff
  - Roast beef, vegetables, redskin potatoes, assorted pie
- Event U menu – Worship Department meeting
  - Lasagna with meat sauce, breadsticks, salad
- UP Café
  - Chicken or ham special, meatball hoagie

Saturday
- Event U menu – Growth Group Leaders meeting
  - Frittata, bacon, home fries, fruit
- Event U menu – Student Ministries car wash
  - Eggs, bacon, sausage, home fries, fruit

Sunday
- Breakfast – 7:30 to 11:45
  - o Special frittata
  - o Buffet – eggs, bacon, home fries, grits, biscuits, sausage, fruit, Danish, muffins, yogurt
- Lunch – noon to 2 pm
  - o Hot roast beef, vegetables, salad
  - o Lasagna, breadstick, salad
  - o Salad bar

Core Items:

- These Core ingredients are the nucleus to flowable menus.

Chicken: used W, Th, chef special F = no shrink

Hamburgers: used W, Th, F, Sun (meat used for lasagna) = no shrink

Potatoes: used W, Th, F, Sat, Sun = no shrink

Fruit: used W, Th, F, Sat, Sun = no shrink

Hot dogs: W, Th, chef special = no shrink

OUR CONTINUED FOCUS

From meal to meal and day to day, we keep our food safe (ie correct temperatures). We utilize any excess product for the next scheduled meals. Our connected menus are planned and executed for a 1-2% acceptable shrink.

CATERING MENU EXAMPLE

God's Chosen People Serving God's Food to God's Family
- List the approximate guest count. _____
- Ministry account # to be charged_____
- Finance: charge credit total to account 651055

  _____

- Total cost – per person unless otherwise indicated.

  _____

Breakfast ala carte	Breakfast Meals
Bagel Tray w/cream cheese and jelly - $.90 pp	Hot Breakfast Buffet (minimum of 20 people) - $4.50 pp
Danish tray (minimum of 6) - $.97 pp	Includes eggs, potatoes, bacon, sausage, English muffins, and fruit
Fresh Seasonal Fruit - $.80 pp	(volunteers for preparation and serving may be needed)
Yogurt Cup $.59 pp	On-Site Hot Breakfast
Frittata (similar to quiche but yummier) (minimum of 12 people) - $1.50 pp	Buffet - $5 (min. of 20 ppl)

Appetizers	Snacks
Cubed cheese tray with crackers and dipping sauce (6 people minimum) - $1.95 pp	Trail mix - $.45 pp
	Assorted 1.5 oz bag chips - $.60 pp
Vegetable Tray with ranch dip (6 people minimum) - $1.42 pp	Granola bars - $.45 pp
Seasonal fresh fruit - $.97 pp	Please indicate where your snacks are needed.

10. Commissioning You

The Food Ministry is so robust and capable that it stepped into the gap for inner city children when COVID-19 struck in 2020. Drive-through free warm lunches were first, followed by delivery to homes via Urban Impact Foundation. Then, they doubled up to warm lunch plus tomorrow's breakfast given to each child. How many? More than 1,000 meals per day. Why? Because that is how God's Chosen People Serve God's Food to God's Family. Is it hard to do? No! Because CONTINUOUS FLOW is SCALEABLE and ROBUST, capable of serving one person or 10,000.

But the message to you from the case study is that you can apply the Principles to your life, your family, your church, your work or your neighborhood by using each step we used for food. Converting each step from food to family, it would be:

- Who are your CUSTOMERS and what are their needs and wants?
- What TASKS are you doing to meet these needs and are you doing them well?
- Are you using TEAMWORK and are you mentoring each other?
- Do your processes FLOW and are they connected in ways that are kind and enabling?

- Do you INVENTORY wisely and is it supportive of the prior four questions?
- Do you solve PROBLEMS with kind mentoring and Problem/Cause/Solution/Action/Measure?
- Is YOUR FLOW balanced and constructive for your family?
- Is YOUR MENU for life proper and are you living it right?
- Is your MENU CONNECTED such that your family thrives?
- Is your SUMMARY that YOU are doing these 9?

Are you willing to put God in all 10 of these? We did and found Him to be an awesome traveling partner. Joe and Richard did and found that they could feed 1,000 people, approaching the 5,000 Jesus fed in Matthew 14:13-21. You can do it. Try a line, then more. Be guided by God's Principles.

About the Author

Keith and Sally Turnbull are a loving couple four years into their fourth generation – old in years yet young in love. So much so that they have Lessons they're compelled to share with you no matter what generation you are now. They learned love to the depth of unconditional as children during the Great Depression and World War II.

Keith is an engineer and scientist whose career advanced to Executive Vice President of Alcoa. Sally majored in business then devoted her life to mentoring children, her five and thousands of others at church.

Keith and Sally are Christians but have written this book for everyone, regardless of your view of God. Love is the story line written with uncommon candor to share with you and the next four generations.

They live at their home next to the lake in Pittsburgh, Pa.

Acknowledgments

My acknowledgement for the book is YOU – the reader. I know that you will find such a choice to be unusual. But Sally and I are two unusual people who have learned and lived unconditional love and yearn to share that with you. Why? Because each tiny step we took in the direction of our book title deepened our love for each other.

That is why Sally encouraged me to open the journals she intended to be private and to share anything she had written with you. Both of us cried as we read them, looked deep into our hearts and, with uncommon candor, gifted their contents to you. Why? Because we believed that you, our precious reader, just might find one takeaway (or perhaps more) that you will take from our Life Story into your life story and thereby improve your life.

Please read our story, our whole story, anticipating there will be such a finding for you. And then, for whatever you now think about the existence or importance of God, know that He was the very source of our unconditional love and He would like to share that love with you.

From the Editor

This journey officially started on October 15, 2019 when my grandfather wrote "The Book" at the top of a yellow legal notepad. Exactly one year later – with a dozen notepads and over 400 handwritten pages – we completed this book together. While I had studied journalism in college, I stepped away to raise kids and to pursue a career in social work while living in another city. When I moved home to Pittsburgh in 2019, this book – long discussed – suddenly became a reality. I am immeasurably grateful to hear their story and to be mentored by my grandfather as we spent hundreds of hours sitting at my grandparents' kitchen table. My kids, Lucy and Paul, now have priceless memories of days spent at the lake, feeding the ducks and looking at family photo albums. His wisdom and humility have always made him a role model in my life, but I never imagined I would receive the intense, challenging, and invaluable one-on-one mentorship of the past year. I am forever changed by it, for the better. God has gifted him with unconditional love, and I pray I will carry forward that love to the next generation.

-Jessica T Weaver
Editor and granddaughter

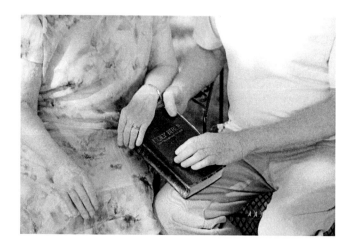